MW01103285

The National Wildlife Federation Book of

FAMILY NATURE ACTIVITIES

OTHER NATIONAL WILDLIFE FEDERATION

BOOKS FROM HENRY HOLT

FOR THE BIRDS!
by Anne Halpin

WILDLIFE WATCHER'S HANDBOOK
by Joe LaTourrette

The National Wildlife Federation Book of

FAMILY NATURE ACTIVITIES

50 SIMPLE PROJECTS AND ACTIVITIES IN THE NATURAL WORLD

Page Chichester

and the National Wildlife Federation

AN OWL BOOK
HENRY HOLT AND COMPANY
NEW YORK

Henry Holt and Company, Inc.
Publishers since 1866
115 West 18th Street
New York, New York 10011

Henry Holt ® is a registered
trademark of Henry Holt and Company, Inc.

Published in Canada by Fitzhenry & Whiteside Ltd.,
195 Allstate Parkway, Markham, Ontario L3R 4T8.

Library of Congress Cataloging-in-Publication Data
Chichester, Page.
The National Wildlife Federation book of family nature activities:
50 simple projects and activities in the natural world/Page Chichester.—1st ed.
p. cm.
Includes bibliographical references (p.) and index.
ISBN 0-8050-4686-0 (alk. paper)
1. Natural history projects. 2. Nature study—Activity programs.
I. National Wildlife Federation. II. Title.
QH55.C48 1997
508--dc21 97-812

Henry Holt books are available for special
promotions and premiums.
For details contact:
Director, Special Markets.

First Edition 1997

Designed by Paula R. Szafranski
Illustrations by Jackie Aher

Printed in the United States of America
All first editions are printed on acid-free paper.∞

1 3 5 7 9 10 8 6 4 2

To all those who share their love of
and knowledge about nature with others

Contents

Foreword

Since its inception more than sixty years ago, the National Wildlife Federation (NWF) has been one of the nation's leading conservation organizations. Over the years, it has assumed leadership positions in a wide variety of critical conservation issues, ranging from the protection of endangered species to the Clean Air and Clean Water acts.

One of the primary avenues for support and information on conservation issues is education. NWF sponsors projects for all school grade levels, from kindergarten through college, reaching tens of thousands of students each year through these direct programs. NWF speaks to tens of thousands more through its educational and entertaining magazines, *Ranger Rick, Your Big Backyard, National Wildlife,* and *International Wildlife.*

With this exciting new book, NWF seeks to broaden its outreach to both children and adults. This guide to outdoor activities is designed for families who want to explore nature together. The activities cover everything from insects to backyard mammals, from recycling to bird feeding. This book will even show you how to build a real igloo, or a live tepee. It allows parents to teach their children about the wonders and perplexities, the mysteries and miracles of nature. Its easy-to-follow instructions enable adults with only a basic understanding of nature to function like skilled naturalists. It turns learning into a family adventure, and fosters a deeper appreciation of the natural world.

During my seventeen years with NWF, I have seen the organization produce many fine products that have made me proud to be a part of the Federation and its endeavors. *The National Wildlife Federation Book of Family Nature Activities* meets the NWF standard of quality. It will provide your family with hours, days, and even months of outdoor fun, excitement, and enrichment.

—***Roy Geiger***
Coordinator, NWF Education Center and Volunteer Programs

Introduction

From my office, I have a clear view of our compost pile. It is in a roofless former garage that is being overtaken by Virginia creeper vine (which the birds love). A birdbath and a feeder occupy one garage windowsill. In the tree above the compost are a birdhouse and an ear of dried corn on a chain, which hangs from a branch. The backyard is graced by a new Kid's Corner (which contains my daughter's garden), a pole-bean tepee, butterfly and bird plantings, several window boxes, the telltale signs of various experiments, and still—for my taste—too much grass.

Inside on the windowsill are a 5-gallon terrarium, a wormatorium, and two wave bottles. In a nearby workroom, the first coat of paint is drying on a bat house, and in the basement, our worm bins need turning, and river- and pond-dipping nets await use.

On our porch, the super-duper insect cage that has hatched three swallowtail butterflies now holds a cocoon of an eight-spotted forester moth and the larva of a cutworm (we suspect). Above the porch is a nesting platform. None of these additions and improvements existed a year ago.

This may sound like a lot, but there's still so much left to do. I'd like to enlarge our butterfly gardens and build a stone wall, among other projects. And I'd love to lose some more grass. Our tiny, apartment-building yard is somewhat limiting, though—it's less than half the size of a typical suburban yard.

Not every project has been an unqualified success. I once spent several hours waiting for a butterfly to emerge from its chrysalis so I could photograph the event. When I returned from a lengthy telephone conversation, the swallowtail was already out and pumping up its wings, no doubt congratulating itself on its timing. No birds have moved into the birdhouse or the nesting platform (although a house wren seems to be advertising for a housemate), and the squirrels have yet to tackle the dried-corn-on-a-chain feeder. Oh well, maybe next year.

On the other hand, there have been many successes. Because I've thought about so many of these projects for so long, accomplishing the task is satisfying. It's a pretty birdhouse, even if it is unoccupied. More birds, butterflies, and other animals are using our yard, and we're enjoying the display. We've even had ruby-throated hummingbirds visit the nasturtiums in my daughter's window box. Not only are my fellow apartment dwellers contributing their kitchen scraps to the compost pile, one of our neighbors has started a second pile. This in a neighborhood where most people still put all garden waste out for the trash collectors.

Most important, my daughter is enjoying the yard more and is anxiously waiting for the tepee to be fully covered with vines. We have explored several habitats beyond our backyard, and we continue to expand our horizons. And while most of our neighbors look on me with what could be generously described as skepticism, many of their sons and daughters have inspected our worm bins and participated in various experiments and activities.

Like my daughter, I grew up fascinated by nature. I was always bringing home snakes, bugs, and crayfish that lived in and around the fields of our 8-acre home. Unlike her, though, I didn't have an adult around to help explain these wonders and guide me in further explorations. My mother, who hoped I'd grow up to be a park ranger, encouraged (or at least did not discourage) me, but her store of natural knowledge was limited. My father's idea of a great outdoor experience was to drive around in the car or go out on a power boat.

So when I left childhood, I left hands-on nature behind for the most part. Work and family left precious little time for outdoor activities. I've spent a lot of time talking about nature, but never doing much about it. True, I've photographed elephants, bears, and other wild animals, and hiked through rain forests and savannas, but I haven't spent much time exploring the workings of nature. It wasn't until recent years that I finally resumed up-close, hands-on nature investigations through writing and photography. The point is that it's never too late, and you're never too old to start.

But don't go it alone. Take your children along. Be a model and a mentor to them. Encourage and invite them to share in outdoor activities and investigations. You can't and shouldn't force them, but if they develop an interest, they will likely carry it with them throughout their lives. As often as not, evidence of parental interest will foster and cement theirs.

These activities will help you and your children connect not only with nature, but with each other. Your children's natural curiosity is bound to revive, inspire, and revitalize your own, and their questions are sure to stump you sometimes. Don't be afraid to say, "I don't know; let's look that one up." The experiences and surprises, successes and failures you share will expand your understanding and appreciation of nature and create fond memories for you both.

—Page Chichester

How to Use This Book

Although most activities stand alone, some of them build on previous ones or require materials made in other activities. The second activity, for instance, incorporates materials created in the first. The Worm-a-rama requires the Habitat for the Harmless container described later in the book. These interdependent activities are cross-referenced in the text, so skip around to your heart's content.

Each activity has been assigned a difficulty level. By necessity, these are subjective, based on the author's skills and on what I considered to be average adult skill levels. They range from Pathfinder (low) to Naturalist (medium) to Explorer (high). These designations are intended as general guidelines.

You may find it useful to practice some activities—such as the twig whistle—before involving your children. Sometimes, it takes a trial run to get it right. Once the first one is done and you see that it toots sweet, demonstrate it to your children and offer to show them how to make one. Pretty soon, you'll be able to crank them out in no time, with each new one sounding better than the last.

Take the Next Step sections expand on activities in one of many possible directions. **Tips and Tidbits** are just that, including not only ideas and suggestions, but fun facts to wow both you and your children. The **Resources** listings in the back of the book offer additional information and contact addresses.

Activities in Part III, Beyond Your Backyard—Going Farther Afield, are less specific and less how-to oriented than those in Parts I and II, allowing for the variations among habitats from region to region. This part encourages you to use some of the knowledge gained and the tools created in the book's first two parts to explore some nearby habitats. Then, when you travel to some of the great national parks, refuges, and other protected natural areas, you will be better equipped to appreciate what each has to offer.

As with any book describing activities, some of which involve power tools, bodies of water, and other potential hazards, some words of caution are in order. The building projects should be completed using utmost care and, where needed, safety equipment such as goggles and masks. Do not collect any animals, plants, or other natural things in state or national parks or other protected areas. Ask permission from the owner before entering or collecting anything on private land.

Given the age and skill ranges of youngsters, I could not begin to suggest who does what in each activity. That is for the parent or other responsible adult to decide. I have taught my 10-year-old how to use a power drill (although she doesn't like the noise). Of course, she also knows not to use it without supervision. Her favorite tool, though, is the hand-powered wood rasp.

Before exploring unfamiliar habitats, learn what safety precautions you may need to take, either from guidebooks or from people familiar with the area. Getting lost, drenched, or bitten is a bad introduction to an area, and could be life-threatening.

Don't expect your children to be wildly excited about each and every activity. Even when they start out fully engaged, sometimes their attention fades in mid-project. Fine, let them go. They'll return in their own time. Even if they don't, they'll have a sense of having been involved, and sometimes that's enough.

And don't expect them to turn the compost, water the flower boxes, and perform all the follow-up that some activities require. Kids will be kids (as they should be), and let's face it, even adults forget (sometimes mistakenly on purpose). You're in this together, and sometimes you the parent will have to do the heavy lifting. Don't push it, and you may be pleasantly surprised by the initiative and attention your children demonstrate.

Feel free to expand on the activities and experiments beyond the **Take the Next Step** suggestions. The most revealing and satisfying discoveries are the result of one's own curiosity. Also, please make use of suggested books or other sources of information listed under **Find Out More** and in the **Further Reading** and **Resources** lists at the end of the book. Space limitations require simplicity, but where nature is concerned, there are few simple answers. Building a bat house is not so complicated, but the reasons why the structure is or is not occupied may be, because they depend on the species of bat (if any) in your neighborhood, the availability of water, the season, the region, and other factors.

When requesting information from any organization or corporation, state your *specific* request clearly and briefly, and include a self-addressed, stamped envelope (SASE). If possible, call first to check on the availability of what you are requesting and to verify the cost (if any), including postage and handling, before sending a check. When ordering from a catalog by phone, follow ordering instructions and have a credit card ready.

Finally, let the publishers hear from you. Parents are their children's first teachers, and it is a lifelong commitment. You know best what works and what doesn't. The author has tested every activity, but there are always better techniques, materials, ideas, and other improvements that could be incorporated. We'd like your input, so that future activity books can be improved.

A Note About Woodworking: Lumber is sold in nominal sizes: 1" x 8", 2" x 2", and so on. Because of shrinkage, the actual size is smaller. Always measure before cutting, and sketch out a plan tailored to your lumber, especially if you change the design.

About the National Wildlife Federation

The mission of the National Wildlife Federation is to educate, inspire, and assist individuals and organizations of diverse cultures to conserve wildlife and other natural resources and to protect the earth's environment for a peaceful, equitable, and sustainable future. As the nation's largest nonprofit wildlife conservation organization, NWF serves a network of more than 5 million grassroots conservationists dedicated to protecting wildlife, wild places, and a healthy environment for people and wildlife alike.

NWF invites and encourages everyone to enjoy the outdoors and join in its preservation through educational outreach programs and publications. Successful programs include NatureLink®, Wildlife Camp®, Teen Adventure, Conservation Summits®, NatureQuest®, Earth Tomorrow®, Campus Outreach®, and Backyard Wildlife Habitat®. Information kits directed to educators include NatureScope®, Animal Tracks®, EarthSavers®, and Wildlife Week®. Our four award-winning magazines are *National Wildlife, International Wildlife, Ranger Rick,* and *Your Big Backyard.* NWF also publishes the *Conservation Directory* of more than 2,000 national and international conservation organizations, both governmental and nongovernmental, and *EnviroAction* newsletter, which provides updates on national environmental legislation.

For more information, call our toll-free number, 800-822-9919, or write to National Wildlife Federation, 8925 Leesburg Pike, Vienna VA 22184-0010.

Acknowledgments

I would like to thank everyone who helped with this book, but that would require another entire book. I therefore will limit myself to those who lent the most recent and direct assistance in the form of information, comments, advice, suggestions, ideas, and time-consuming reviews. Without their help, this book would not exist.

Mary Appelhof, the Worm Woman of Kalamazoo; Margaret Barker and Tim Dillon at the Cornell Laboratory of Ornithology; Bob Benson, Public Information Officer, Bat Conservation International; Gary Dunn, Education Director, Young Entomologists' Society, Inc.; Carrol Henderson, Nongame Wildlife Supervisor, Minnesota Department of Natural Resources; Dr. David Orcutt, Professor of Plant Physiology, Virginia Polytechnic Institute and State University; Bret Rappaport, President, Wild Ones Landscapers; David Schmidt, Outreach Coordinator, Global Rivers Environmental Education Network (GREEN); Bill Tikkala, Special Projects Forester, American Forests; Kyle Weaver, Stackpole Books. Many others at conservation and educational organizations also were generous with their knowledge and information.

I also owe a debt of gratitude to many people at the National Wildlife Federation. These include Craig Tufts, Chief Naturalist and Manager of NWF's Backyard Wildlife Habitat® Program; Susan Johnson, Director of Environmental Education; Barbara Farley, Senior Coordinator, NWF Conservation Summits®; Tara Wintermeyer, Coordinator of Youth Programs; Glen Nelson, NatureQuest® Teen Adventure coordinator; Sharon Levy, Librarian; and Roger DiSilvestro, Senior Editor, *National Wildlife* and *International Wildlife* magazines, who coordinated this project.

Perhaps the most appreciation should go to my family. A. Lee Chichester and Jack Russell not only helped research and review several activities, but also provided many good examples and photographic subjects, as well as suggestions and encouragement. Katharina Lee Chichester was not only a patient model and a gifted artistic collaborator, but also an enthusiastic guinea pig for numerous activities, projects, and experiments. K. Ini Chichester lent much-needed moral, logistical, and editorial support, in addition to an admirable level of faith, patience, and understanding during what, at times, seemed to be a never-ending project.

PART I

Knowing and Improving Your Habitat

Wildlife Gardening

CREATE A "BEFORE" PICTURE

LEVEL: Explorer (high; about 2 hours)

SEASONS: All

MATERIALS:
Graph paper
Pencil and eraser
Yardstick or tape measure

OPTIONAL
Garden guide to common plant types Colored pens or pencils

INTRODUCTION

Much of the first part of this book will focus on learning about your backyard habitat and improving it for wildlife. A broad name for these activities is wildlife gardening, which follows many of the same methods as traditional gardening, but focuses on wildlife needs as well as aesthetics. This approach will improve the habitat for you and your family as well, because you will have more firsthand opportunities to view and study wildlife.

Turning a typical lawn into a miniature refuge for wildlife takes time. You should see improvements within the first year, but a serious makeover will take several years, and it never really ends. Every year brings new surprises and gradual changes, and if you document the progress, you will be amazed at the long-term improvements.

Gardening for wildlife also takes a lot of work, but the benefits are many. Not only will you have more wildlife to watch, study, and admire, you'll be helping wildlife survive. Besides, if you enjoy gardening, it won't seem like hard labor.

Word about good habitat travels quickly among wild animals. The first ones likely to notice the improvements in your backyard are the birds and the butterflies. A healthy bird population seems to be a sign to other animals: Safe stomping grounds here. Even small suburban plots can attract and harbor rabbits, turtles, lizards, chipmunks, and other wild creatures.

In addition, by taking a more nature-minded approach to gardening—including composting and planting native species—you can decrease or eliminate your use of expensive chemical fertilizers and pesticides, improving the quality of your air and groundwater. Finally, by replacing high-maintenance lawn grass with low-maintenance flowers, vines, shrubs, and trees, you'll be able to spend less time mowing the lawn and more time enjoying your yard and the wildlife it attracts.

With luck, your backyard improvements will inspire a neighbor or two to do the same, increasing the refuge's area. Imagine if a whole neighborhood joined the movement: your community could become a miniature greenway, providing improved living spaces for both people and wildlife.

In this activity, not only will you hone mapmaking skills, you'll gain a clear overview of your garden and learn what kinds of plants are in it. This will help you to see what your lawn offers in the way of wildlife habitat and what needs improvement. These are the first steps to turning your backyard into a backyard habitat.

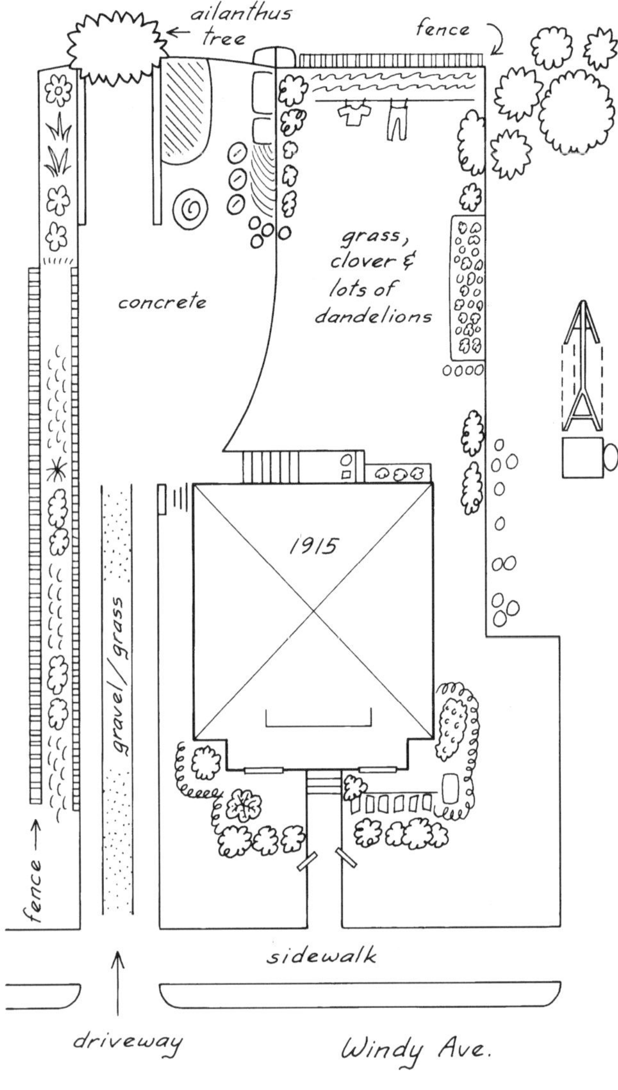

Example of a first-draft map

STEPS

1. Use graph paper to make a detailed bird's-eye-view (aerial) map of your yard. You needn't be exact to the millimeter, but try to make your picture roughly to scale.

   Start with the perimeter and add major elements—house, garage, sheds, other outbuildings, driveway, sidewalks, roads, trees, and any creeks or streams. Then fill in the garden plots and shrubs. Include bird feeders or baths, if you have them. Unless someone in your family is an experienced mapmaker, expect to make at least two maps—one rough draft, and the other more finished. Depending on your family's mapmaking skills, you may need to do more. Be sure to include an arrow pointing north; this will provide an orientation and help you decide where to plant new garden plots later.
2. In one corner, list the lot's approximate square footage (or acreage) and the average amount of time it takes to mow the lawn. In the other corner, date and label the map "Our House," and add your street address and list the names of all family members.
3. When everyone is satisfied with the drawing, take it to a copy service and make two enlargements—the bigger, the better (18 × 24 inches is a good size). Label one copy "Before." The other will be revised to make an "After" version of your backyard—the "dream" garden described in the next activity.
4. On the "Before" map, label all buildings, trees, bushes, and shrubs. In the garden plots, list the vines, flowers, ground cover, and other plants. If you know what variety of grass your lawn is composed of, include that. Don't bother listing plant types in the vegetable garden unless you plant the same ones every year.
5. Have the family photographer take some pictures of the yard. These will complement your map and can be glued to its borders as visual aids. Your junior cartographers can add color to the finished map. You may want to frame it for display and future reference, or fold it and put it into a pocket of your Backyard Habitat Album (see box in next activity).

Find Out More

See Craig Tufts and Peter Loewer, *Gardening for Wildlife. How to Create a Beautiful Backyard Habitat for Birds, Butterflies and Other Wildlife* (Emmaus, PA: Rodale Press, 1995).

Tips and Tidbits

Good habitat that harbors a diversity of wildlife is more interesting for kids than comparatively monotonous expanses of grass.

By one estimate, if you put all of America's grass-covered lawns together, their combined size would equal that of Michigan. Another estimate puts the combined area of American lawns at 32,000 square miles, somewhat larger than the state of Maine. Make a goal of reducing the amount of grass in your backyard by at least half.

DESIGN A DREAM GARDEN

LEVEL: Naturalist (medium; about 1 hour)

SEASONS: All

MATERIALS:

Enlarged photocopies of your backyard "Before" map (from previous activity)
Paper
Pencil
Scissors
Removable-glue stick, self-sticking notes, or tracing paper

INTRODUCTION

The next step toward improved habitat is envisioning a backyard that is more attractive to wildlife and redesigning it on paper as your "After" map. Your dream garden should include areas friendly to as many different creatures as possible: butterflies and other insects, birds, amphibians, reptiles, and mammals (both nonhuman and human). Good habitat provides food, water, shelter, and safe places to raise young. These are the four basic requirements for wildlife survival. Come to think of it, humans share these same minimum requirements.

STEPS

1. Study your "Before" map, looking for things that make good habitat. These include trees, both dead and alive, shrubs, tangled vines, brush piles, open areas, overgrown thickets, and such. Label these on your "After" drawing; they will form the foundation of your new backyard.
2. Think about what is missing in your habitat. Do you have bird feeders and/or food-bearing trees and bushes? Is water available? Do you have a butterfly garden? Bird, squirrel, and bat houses? How about a nice stone wall? What about a compost pile? If you already have some of these, think about how they could be expanded or improved. Can you live with a little less lawn? A carpet of grass doesn't make very good habitat for most animals. Diversity is the key: the more habitat types you offer, the more wildlife you're likely to attract.
3. Make cutouts representing missing pieces of your habitat. Using removable glue or self-sticking notes, arrange the various habitat elements. Alternatively, you can use sheets of tracing paper to make different versions. It might help if each family member pretends to be a different kind of animal, looking at the map and making suggestions from a wildlife standpoint.
4. Color the "After" version and hang it next to "Before," or put them both in your Backyard Habitat Album (see box). Many of the following activities will help you turn your backyard into this dream garden. As you improve your backyard, update your drawing by permanently attaching the new additions and noting the date of completion.

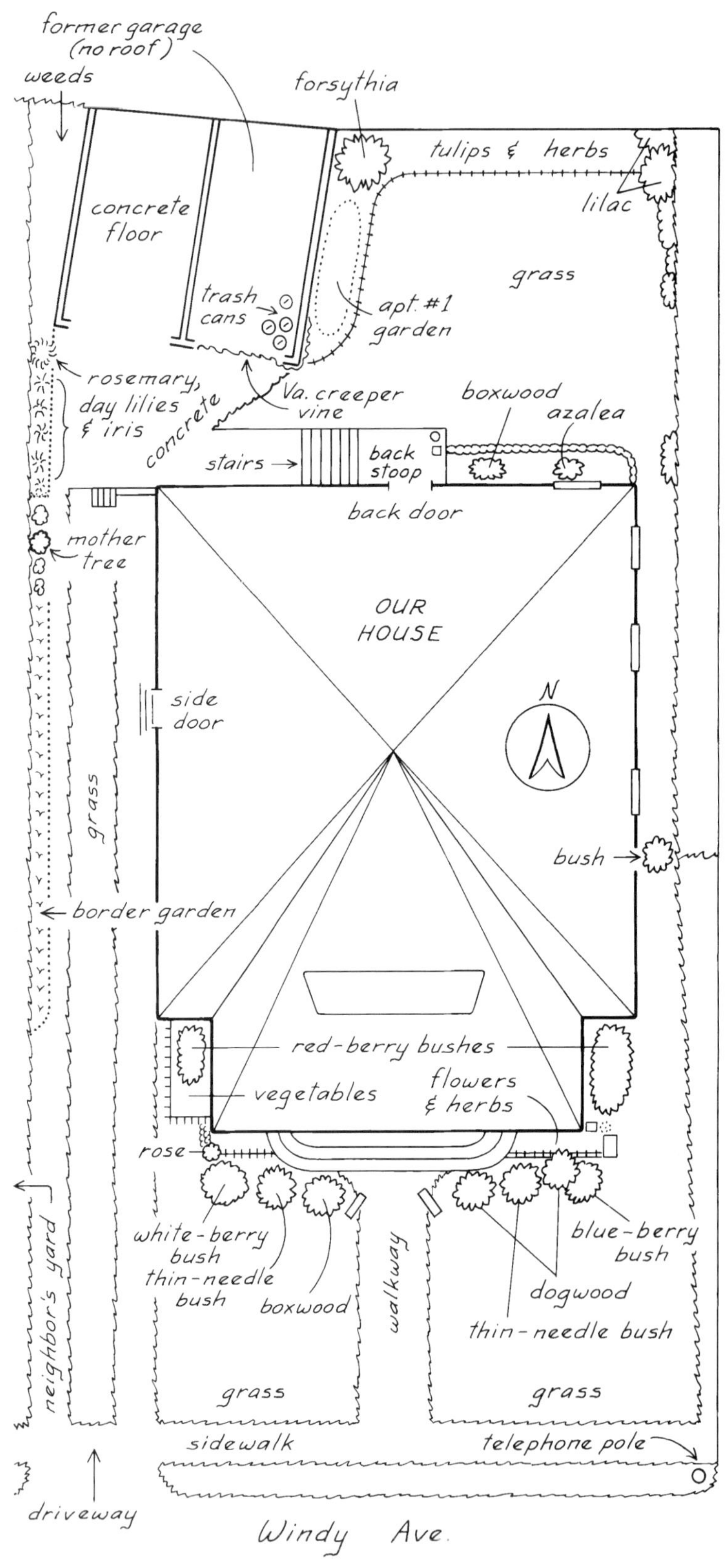

"Before" and "After" versions of a backyard habitat map

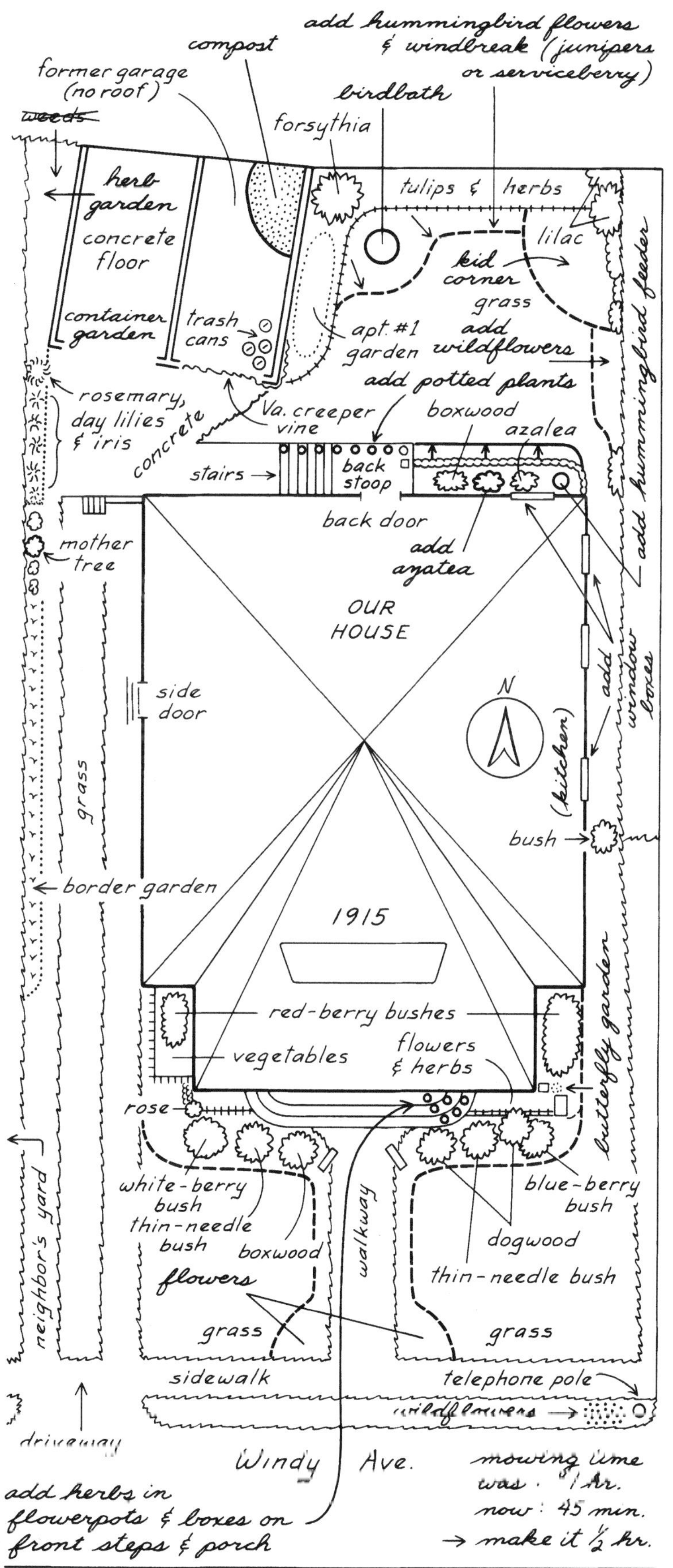

add hummingbird flowers
& windbreak (junipers
or serviceberry)
compost
former garage
(no roof)
weeds
birdbath
forsythia
herb
garden
concrete
floor
tulips & herbs
lilac
kid
corner
grass
container
garden
trash
cans
apt. #1
garden
add
wildflowers
add hummingbird feeder
rosemary,
day lilies
& iris
add potted plants
Va. creeper
vine
boxwood
azalea
concrete
stairs
back
stoop
back door
add
azalea
mother
tree
OUR
HOUSE
side
door
N
add
window
boxes
(kitchen)
grass
bush
border garden
1915
red-berry bushes
vegetables
flowers
& herbs
butterfly garden
rose
white-berry
bush
thin-needle
bush
boxwood
blue-berry
bush
dogwood
thin-needle bush
walkway
neighbor's yard
flowers
grass
grass
sidewalk
telephone pole
wildflowers
driveway
Windy Ave.
mowing time
was: 1 hr.
now: 45 min.
→ make it ½ hr.
add herbs in
flowerpots & boxes on
front steps & porch

Make a Backyard Habitat Album

This can be a three-ring binder, a photo album, a journal with blank pages, or whatever works best for you. The idea is to document the progress of this long-term, habitat-improvement project. Ask the artist in the family to make a picture for the cover or title page. Encourage every family member to write a paragraph about the garden—memories, what they like or dislike about it. As you work through the backyard-habitat activities that follow, take pictures and add them to the album. Reflections on the project can be added from time to time as well. Don't forget to make a guest list of the wildlife visitors your habitat attracts.

Improving your backyard habitat requires knowledge of the animals you want to attract. Think of this as an ongoing educational process and try to review and revise your dream garden plan at least once or twice a year. As a reminder, revisit the map on the day you reset the clocks each year or on the first day of fall and the first day of spring.

FIND OUT MORE

See Craig Tufts, *The Backyard Naturalist* (Vienna, VA: National Wildlife Federation, 1997). This 80-page book gives specific suggestions for creating a place for wildlife. The author oversees NWF's Backyard Wildlife Habitat® Program, which has certified and registered more than 17,000 backyard habitats across the country. Tufts has spent the past 10 years turning his 9,000-square-foot backyard in suburban northern Virginia into lush habitat for wildlife.

The book is part of an information packet including the 12-page planning and planting booklet *Backyard Wildlife Habitat,* a good first source with a bibliography for further reading. To order the modestly priced package, write to National Wildlife Federation, Backyard Wildlife Habitat Program, 8925 Leesburg Pike, Vienna VA 22184. For credit-card orders, call 800-432-6564.

Tips and Tidbits

A diverse habitat area with sources of food, water, and shelter can double the number of animals that visit your backyard.

Creating a sanctuary for wildlife can significantly increase the value of your property.

Set Up a Kids' Corner

LEVEL: Can be tailored for any level

SEASONS: Spring and summer

MATERIALS:
Paper and colored markers for making a certificate

OPTIONAL
Wooden stakes
Permanent markers or paint
String

INTRODUCTION

One way to give your children a greater sense of ownership and involvement in their backyard wildlife habitat is to cede them a section of the yard to do with as they please (within reason). Although most kids already consider the home yard theirs, too few are invited to make important design decisions. The idea of a personal piece of property can be attractive for a youngster.

STEPS

1. Select an appropriate site. If you mapped your yard in the earlier activity, you may have already found an ideal area for a Kids' Corner. If not, walk around the property with your youngsters and look for several possible sites. In choosing the final location, try to decide on a first-year project. Some projects—such as letting an area go wild—do not require full sunlight; others—such as planting a butterfly or vegetable garden—do.
2. Choose a size. Deciding on a project and a location will help determine how big to make the plot. Other considerations are the number, ages, and motivation levels of your children. A wild area can be overseen by younger children, because it needs little or no maintenance. A vegetable garden, on the other hand, is more demanding. Don't give them too much area at first. If the experiment is successful, you can enlarge it next year.
3. It is important that the whole family abide by the land-grant agreement—no unauthorized weeding, mowing, or other interference. Parents should be facilitators, consultants, cheerleaders, and occasional helpers in the process.

   This agreement can be formalized with a certificate of ownership and a small, dinnertime ceremony. As part of the formalities, add the

Digging a Kids' Corner garden

area to your dream garden map, and include a project description in your Backyard Habitat Album. You may want to mark the area with stakes, bearing your kids' names in ink or paint.

Project Ideas

The easiest project is to just let the area go wild. Don't touch it for at least a year or two. This creates both a no-maintenance garden plot and a study in succession, as cultivated grasses and plants give way to hardier, more successful competitors. This wild patch will also provide cover for birds and small mammals. For a more complete example of succession, let the area go untouched for five years or so.

The downside is that your neighbors and local government may frown on such weedy proliferations. Two other considerations: Succession isn't always pretty—it looks (and is) unruly. Also, your kids may find this project boring—they may want to be more actively involved with their private chunk of land.

More challenging and involving projects include planting wildflowers, herbs, and other bird- or butterfly-gardening plants; setting up a bird-feeding area; or making a brush pile or a composting station.

Don't forget that reducing your lawn area is one of the goals of backyard habitat improvement. A large expanse of manicured lawn requires lots of work and water, and it doesn't offer wildlife much in the way of food and cover. Think of it as a green desert. Your goal is to increase diversity and decrease monoculture (large areas of single-species plants). Many lawn-replacement projects are detailed in later activities.

Find Out More

See Stevie Daniels, *The Wild Lawn Handbook: Alternatives to the Traditional Front Lawn* (New York: Macmillan, 1995); and Ken Druse, *The Natural Habitat Garden* (New York: Clarkson Potter, 1994).

Tips and Tidbits

In some areas, weed ordinances forbid unruly or wild-looking, unmowed gardens. A few go-natural gardeners have also been fined. But many property owners have fought back and changed the outdated local laws. There's even a Chicago attorney who specializes in helping activists rewrite or repeal these restrictions. For more information, write his nonprofit membership organization, Wild Ones Natural Landscapers, at PO Box 23576, Milwaukee WI 53223-0576.

On average, a ⅓-acre grass lawn requires 9,000 gallons of water a week, or more than 100,000 gallons a summer.

Outdoor Composting

LEVEL: Naturalist (medium; about 1 hour set-up)

SEASONS: Spring, summer, fall, and mild winter

MATERIALS:
Shovel or pitchfork
Yard waste (leaves, grass clippings, branches, and twigs)

OPTIONAL
Kitchen waste (no meat, fat, or dairy products)

INTRODUCTION

Yard waste—including grass clippings, twigs, and leaves—is an abundant natural resource around most homes, especially in summer and fall. Unfortunately, many people don't recognize the potential. They recycle newspapers, glass, and plastic containers, but they bag and throw away recyclable plant products.

Create your own backyard composting center. Adding compost to soil replaces important nutrients and increases its capacity to absorb and retain water. It reduces or eliminates the need for chemical fertilizers. Plus, you'll enjoy a window on the process of decomposition and a good complement to your worm-composting project (see next activity).

Composting can be a simple task or a labor-intensive ordeal. Entire books have been written on methods, containers, final-product uses, and even the philosophy of composting. Don't let it become an obsession.

STEPS

1. Find an appropriate site. Location is everything. Your composting center should be close to the garden, but discreet enough not to annoy the neighbors. Avoid a spot that gets direct sunlight all day—this may overcook your compost, killing the decomposer organisms.
2. For mass quantities of yard waste, use the pile-on method. Start with a thin foundation of twigs and branches covered by 6 inches of leaves and grass clippings.
3. Add a thin layer of soil, manure, or compost activator, which you can buy from gardening stores. This ensures an abundance of microbes for the all-important job of decomposing the plant matter.
4. Water generously.
5. Top this with another thin layer of twigs, clippings, and soil, water it, and repeat the process until your pile is at least 3 feet tall. The kids can

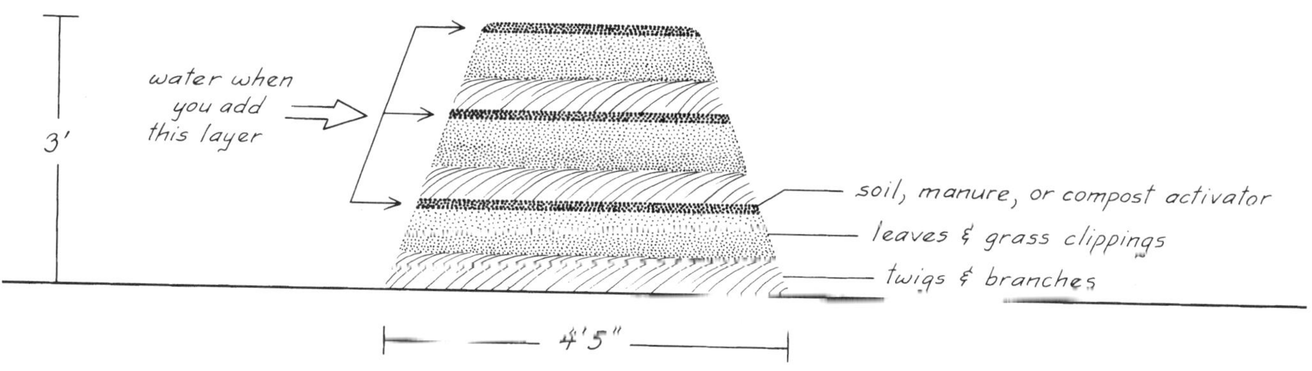

Building an outdoor compost pile. The pile should be at least 3' × 3' × 3'.

help gather and break up twigs, and they can perform the task of mulching the leaves simply by playing in them.

Long Term

If you don't have much in the way of building materials, gradually add them to the pile throughout the summer and fall. Water the pile generously and cover with a tarp to help keep in moisture. Check the compost from time to time to ensure that it hasn't dried out.

Over the next few months, the pile will become a hotbed of activity as bacteria, fungi, worms, insects, and other creatures break down the pile's organic matter. The heat generated by millions of microbes builds up because of the insulating properties of the compost pile. Temperatures in a compost heap can reach 150°F or higher, although the ideal temperature is around 120°F. This is sufficient to kill seeds, weed roots, and other undesirables.

Turning the compost heap keeps it aerated and active.

Kids find this natural-oven aspect fascinating, especially in wintertime. When it's really cooking, give them a thermometer so they can measure just how hot it is near the center.

As the microbial work progresses, the pile will shrink by about half. In spring, mix the finished product with the soil in your garden beds. Be sure to leave a remnant to activate your next compost pile.

If you want a more hands-on approach, turn the pile at least once a month to circulate air and prevent smelly, slow-working anaerobic bacteria from taking over. Good air circulation encourages speedy decomposition. If the temperature rises above 150°F, poke holes in the pile, insert ventilation pipes, or water it. You can also add kitchen scraps: dig a hole in the pile, add the scraps, chop and mix them with the compost, and cover them up.

Some people use containers for composting. These include wooden, brick, or chicken-wire pens; garbage cans; and 55-gallon barrels. Others prefer to buy compost bins, some of which can be cranked for easier turning. Good composters produce several batches a year. Some people add lime to neutralize acidity, especially if they are composting pine needles or other evergreen material, which tends to be acidic.

Take the Next Step

Experiment with your compost by planting three seeds or seedlings in 6-inch pots. Marigold seeds are hardy and fast-growing. Fill one pot with poor, sandy soil; one with backyard soil; and one with backyard soil mixed with an equal amount of compost. Make sure that they all get the same amount of sunlight. You may notice that the compost-enriched soil needs to be watered less often. See which plants grow better.

FIND OUT MORE

See Stu Campbell, *Let It Rot! The Gardener's Guide to Composting* (Pownal, VT: Storey Communications, 1990); and Grace Gershuny and Deborah L. Martin, eds., *The Rodale Book of Composting* (Emmaus, PA: Rodale Press, 1992).

See also the **Resources** listing, page 123.

Tips and Tidbits

Studies suggest that compost can help prevent some common plant diseases, cutting down the need for harmful chemicals. One explanation: well-composted soil is full of oxygen and nutrients, and it holds water well, so plants are less likely to be weakened by lack of food or water. A strong, healthy plant is better able to resist disease.

If your compost doesn't heat up enough to kill stray seeds, you may find surprises—such as "stealth pumpkins"—growing in your garden.

WORM COMPOSTING

LEVEL: Naturalist (medium; about 1½ hours)

SEASONS: All

MATERIALS:

10-gallon container (24" × 16" × 8¾") with lid
Newspaper (about 200 pages)
1 pound redworms (about 1,000 individuals)
Brace and bit or power drill with 1" to 2" bit
Fine screen or mesh
Waterproof glue or heavy-duty tape
Scissors
Three-pronged gardening hand tool
Handful of soil

INTRODUCTION

These days, nearly everyone recycles bottles, cans, and newspapers, but many people still trash their kitchen scraps. These can be composted using nature's little recycling machines, worms. Worm composting turns scraps into fertilizer for your garden or houseplants. Other benefits: you won't have to take out the trash quite so often, what you take out will emit fewer noxious odors and fluids, and you'll reduce the load at your local landfill.

The scientific name for worm composting is *vermicomposting;* the final product is *vermicompost,* which contains worm castings (excrement), decomposing bedding, and organic matter. *Vermi* comes from the Latin word for worm.

The only worms suitable for composting are the scrappy redworms, also known as manure worms or red wigglers. Ask for them by name—nightcrawlers and other earthworms don't do leftovers. Some bait shops and garden supply stores sell redworms, or you can order them from the address given in the **Resources** listing, page 123.

Worm bin with newspaper strips

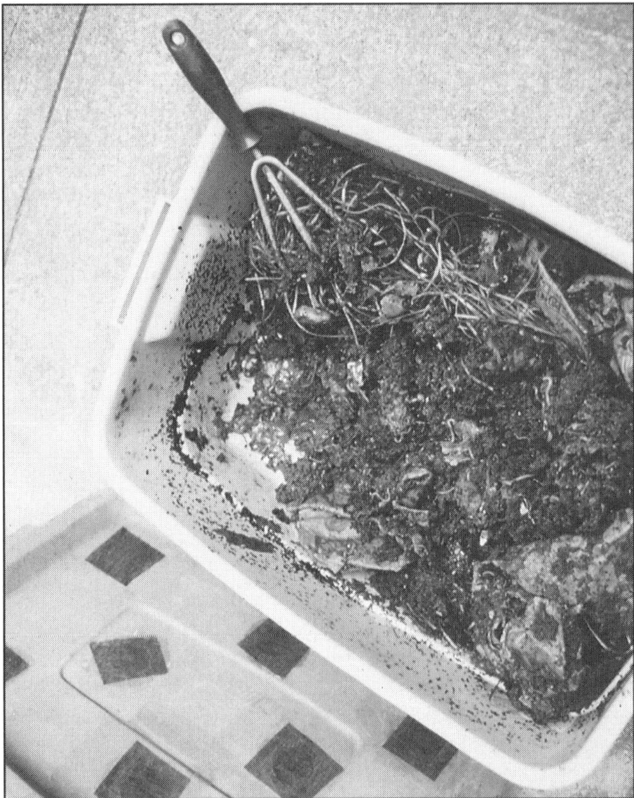

A working worm bin should smell earthy. Bad odors mean something's wrong.

Worm composting offers a firsthand look at how decomposition works. Bins are especially valuable during winter, when temperatures may be too cold for outdoor composting.

STEPS

1. A good beginner's container is Rubbermaid's 10-gallon plastic storage bin. Drill two holes in the top and one hole 2 inches above the bottom on all sides. If you use a small bit, such as 1 inch, drill twice as many holes.
2. Cover each hole with a circle of fine screen or mesh and glue or tape in place on the outside.
3. Take about 200 full sheets (5 lbs.) of newspaper, tear them into inch-wide strips, and put them in the bin. Fluff them up and add water. Squeeze water out until strips are like a moist sponge—damp but not dripping.
4. Spread bedding, and sprinkle with a heaping handful of soil—grit for the worms' gizzards.
5. Now your worm bin is ready for occupancy. Add kitchen scraps, distribute worms among the scraps, cover everything with bedding, and close the lid.

Worms like a moist, dark environment, with temperatures between 55° and 85°F. Keep them in the basement, under the kitchen sink, or in any other accessible location. Your worms will eat nearly half their weight every day; they even eat the newspaper. A thousand worms (about a pound) can gobble up about 3 pounds of food scraps a week.

LONG TERM

Add more scraps as the worm food disappears—you'll gradually develop a feeding rhythm. Replenish the bedding from time to time. If a brown liquid accumulates, soak it up with dry newspaper strips, or use it to water your houseplants. Your bin shouldn't require much work, and it can last for years. It may not be completely odor-free, but the smell should be earthy rather than icky. Bad smells usually mean something's wrong. Turn your worms from time to time with a three-pronged garden digging tool to maintain a healthy air supply.

At least once or twice a year, remove the finished product—rich worm castings. The easiest method is to take out all but a third of your bin's contents and fill the container with fresh bedding. Add the compost that you removed to garden soil or mix it into your outdoor compost pile (see previous activity).

Keeping Your Worms Happy: Care and Feeding

Don't feed your scrap slaves bones or anything fatty or pickled.

Worms will eat meat, but the rotting material will smell bad and may attract rodents and other pests. Composting meat is not recommended.

If you compost meat, make your bin rodent resistant (some counties require this, regardless).

Eggshells will disappear faster if you dry and crush them.

Your bin may harbor fruit flies, so choose its

placement carefully. To help control fruit flies, keep your scrap piles covered with several inches of shredded newspaper or a layer of folded newspaper sections.

Other compost critters may appear in your bin. Except for centipedes and ants, almost all typical residents are worm-friendly and harmless to you.

FIND OUT MORE

See the **Resources** listing, page 123.

Tips and Tidbits

To visit Worm World, part of "the yuckiest site on the Internet," go to New Jersey Online's home page at http://www.nj.com/yucky/worm.

MAKE A WORM-A-RAMA

LEVEL: Naturalist (medium; about 1 hour)

SEASONS: All

MATERIALS:

Habitat for the Harmless observatory (see page 57 for instructions)
Sand or gravel
Potting soil
Compost from your garden
Redworms, also known as red wigglers or manure worms (get them from your worm-composting bin; see previous activity)
Kitchen scraps
Dark cloth to cover observatory (worms prefer darkness)

INTRODUCTION

Redworms are just one of nature's many lean, mean recycling machines. What they eat passes through their long intestines and comes out as castings, an earthy-smelling manure that makes excellent fertilizer. In a composting bin, redworms can help your family reduce the amount of trash that goes to the local landfill by 250 pounds a year or more. This activity enables you to observe this process up close.

Habitat for the Harmless filled with soil

STEPS

1. Fill the bottom inch of your observatory with gravel or sand. Add about 5 inches of potting soil and 5 inches of compost, leaving an inch or two at the top.
2. Water just enough to make the soil moist, but not soggy.
3. Add a few vegetable scraps to the top layer, and put in 20 or so redworms. Cover with a lid and a dark cloth.

LONG TERM

Check your worms every week or so, adding food and

Nightcrawlers require different food from redworms.

water from time to time. You'll be able to watch your worms eat and squirm through the compost and soil. You may even see two worms intertwined in a mating dance. Each worm has both male and female sex organs, so, after mating, a cocoon forms around both worms' middle bands. It will slip off to form a tiny, lemon-shaped ball, which gradually darkens. In three weeks, up to five baby worms will emerge.

When watching worms, shield them from direct light, which they can sense even though they lack eyes. With a little care, you can keep your observatory going for a year or more. You can also add other kinds of worms, but they'll need different foods. Nightcrawlers like green leaves; garden-variety earthworms get their nutrition from the soil they eat. When you're finished, dump everything but the rocks into the family worm bin or compost pile.

Tips and Tidbits

Burrowing worms aerate the soil by creating tunnels that help roots get more air and moisture.

In the wild, worms probably live only a year or so. In captivity, though, a worm may live four or five years.

Redworms have both male and female sex organs. Mature worms can produce more than 130 young in six months—800 can multiply to 150,000 within just six months.

SPROUT A SNACK

LEVEL: Pathfinder (low; ½ hour or less set-up, five days to harvest)

SEASONS: All, but especially fun in winter

MATERIALS:

Quart jar (or 8-ounce jelly jar) with lid, preferably two-part canning type, or use a rubber band to hold the gauze

Seeds available in health food stores: alfalfa, barley, buckwheat, garden cress, garden peas, lentil, mung, mustard, oats, radish, sesame, soy, sunflower, or wheat, among others; also corn kernels and large beans, such as garbanzo, kidney, lima, navy, and pinto beans, which are not usually eaten raw, but cooked

Gauze, nylon stocking, or fine plastic screen or mesh

INTRODUCTION

Few activities are more satisfying than tending live, green plants, especially in the dead of winter. The color green represents the otherwise hidden promise of spring.

One of the benefits of indoor gardening—aside from getting a jump on spring—is enjoying the end result, such as a flower, herb, or vegetable. But that payoff may not come for many weeks or months.

For a crash course in the joys of germination, sprout some edible seedlings as a garnish for salads. This takes only a few days. Besides providing the agricultural equivalent to instant gratification, it demonstrates what happens to seeds underground, before we can see them, and shows what seeds need to germinate and begin growth. For best results, start with fast-growing alfalfa seeds.

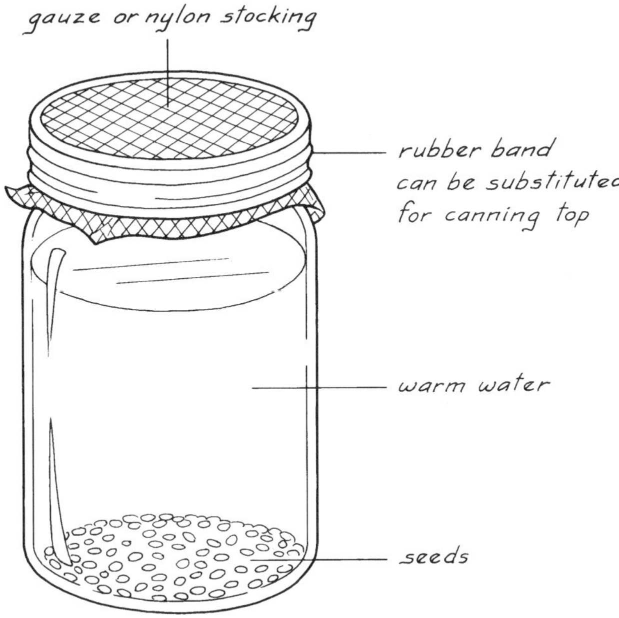

Prepared 8-ounce sprout jar

STEPS

1. Add about a tablespoon of seeds to a clean, quart-sized glass jar and fill it with warm water to within an inch of the top. If some seeds float to the top, stir them until they sink. For a smaller crop, use an 8-ounce jelly jar and a teaspoon of seeds.
2. Cover the jar with nylon, fine screen, or two layers of gauze, and screw on the open-ring part of the lid to hold it. If you don't have canning lids, use a rubber band.
3. Let the seeds soak overnight. In the morning, drain and rinse them with warm water. Pour out the water and put the jar on its side in a warm, dark place, rinsing once or twice daily for the next two or three days until the seeds sprout. Some sprouts need more water, so if you notice your seeds are drying out, rinse more often.
4. After the seeds sprout, place the jar in indirect light until green leaves appear in a day or so, and your healthy snack is ready to eat.
5. To get rid of the seed shells, immerse the sprouts in water and gently shake; the shells (and probably some sprouts) should float to the surface. Use sprouts in salads, as garnish, or as an appetizer. Dip them in salad dressing (or make your own).

TAKE THE NEXT STEP

Experiment to see what conditions are best for germinating some seeds. Use alfalfa seeds in five cups or jelly jars with a ¼-inch layer of cotton in the bottom. Cotton makeup pads work well for this purpose. Label the jars 1 through 5. Put three cups in indirect sun, but give them different amounts of water—moisten the cotton in cup number 1, keep cup number 2 dry, and fill number 3 halfway, keeping the seeds underwater.

Water cups 4 and 5 lightly and put number 4 in the refrigerator and number 5 in a warm, dark place. Every day, lightly water all but the dry cup. After a week, see which are the best conditions for germinating these seeds.

Within three weeks, the plants in cup number 1

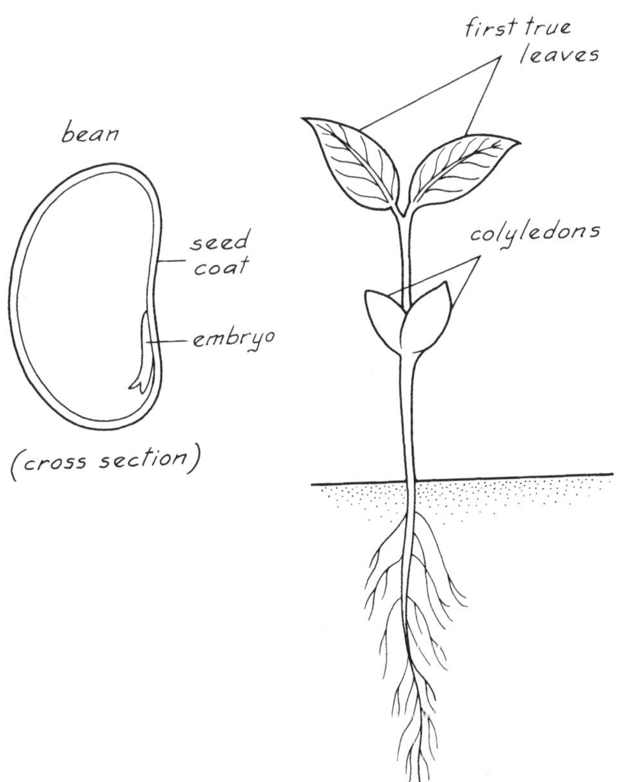

Parts of a seed

Cress sprouts in decorated eggshell

should be about 3 inches tall. Take them out of the container, cut them at the base with scissors and sprinkle the sprouts over your salad.

Find Out More

See "Grow Your Own Vegetable Sprouts," EC 1358, available by sending a 50-cent check to Publication Orders, Extension and Station Communications, A422 Kerr Administration Building, Oregon State University, Corvallis OR 97331-2119.

Tips and Tidbits

Every seed has the following parts: seed coat, endosperm, and embryo; the first leaves that a seed produces are cotyledons, which are actually the seed sides and are filled with food.

Sprouts are low in calories and fat, and high in vitamins A and C, iron, magnesium, and other nutrients. They have been used in the Orient for some 5,000 years.

Cress seeds usually do best on a bed of moist cotton.

Grow an Avocado-Seed Tree

LEVEL: Pathfinder (low; ½ hour or less set-up)

SEASONS: All, but especially fun in winter

MATERIALS:
Avocado pit
Glass
Three toothpicks
Planting pot (6" tall)
Potting soil
Sand
Gravel

INTRODUCTION

Trees have a long life span, so planting one is a little different from planting seasonal crops. In one of his comic strips, *Peanuts* creator Charles Schultz said that planting a tree shows faith in the future. It also implies a commitment to care for the tree. But the rewards are many. Over the years, children may develop a special relationship with their tree, almost as if it were a pet.

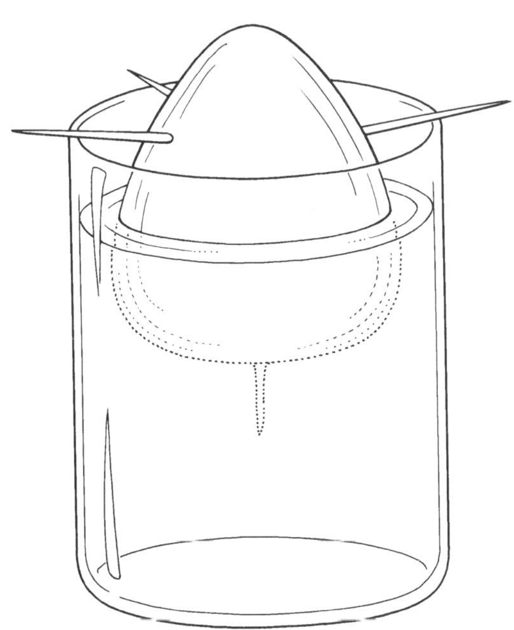

Avocado seed with toothpicks and emerging root

STEPS

1. Avocado seeds can be sprouted several ways. Sometimes you can find one with the root already poking out. With one of these, carefully wash it with tap water, peel off the brown outer skin, plant in sandy soil with the pointed (top) end sticking out of the soil about an inch, water regularly, and hope for the best. If you compost with worms (see activity on page 13), you may be able to find sprouted seeds in your bin.
2. For a seed with no visible root, wash it, peel off the skin, and insert three toothpicks about halfway between the middle and the pointed end.
3. Put this in a cup or jar with the toothpicks resting on the rim and fill the container with water until the rounded, bottom third of the seed is covered.
4. Put the container in a warm, dark location. Change the water weekly.
5. In a month or so, the root should be visible. When the roots are well developed and a growth shoot appears at the top, transfer the seed to a pot at least 6 inches tall and filled with sandy soil with a layer of gravel in the bottom. Leave the seed's top inch sticking up, and move it to a sunny location. Keep it well watered, because avocados like moist—though not soggy—soil.

Avocado seed propagation doesn't always work, so try two or more at once. After the plant has grown at least a foot tall and has several leaves, pinch off the top 2 inches (this is called "topping") to encourage branches to grow, making for a bushier tree.

Peat Moss Method

If the toothpick method fails, try putting a pit into a plastic bag filled halfway with moist peat moss. The peat moss should be about as moist as a damp sponge, but not dripping wet. Don't close the bag tightly, but rather fold the top over and place it in a warm, dark area, where you won't forget it. Check it after a few weeks.

FIND OUT MORE

See Millicent Selsam and Deborah Peterson, *The Don't Throw It, Grow It Book of Houseplants* (New York: Random House, 1977) (out of print; look for it in your local library).

Tips and Tidbits

Florida avocados are usually larger and easier to germinate; those from California are more stubborn.

Avocados are native to Central and South America. They also are known as "alligator pears."

Set Up a Terrarium

LEVEL: Pathfinder (low; 1 hour set-up)

SEASONS: All, but especially fun in winter

MATERIALS:

Large, clear glass or plastic container with a wide opening (container should hold 1 gallon or more and be about 8 tall, either upright or on its side); an unused aquarium with a glass top may also be used

Watertight stopper/cover (glass, cork, plastic wrap and rubber band, etc.)

Small plants that do not need direct sunlight (see list)

Sterile potting soil

Sand

Crushed charcoal (available at aquarium supply stores, or use barbecue charcoal, but not the match-lighting kind)

Gravel or pebbles

INTRODUCTION

For all practical purposes, our planet is a closed system, which means that all the water, air, and natural resources in it are irreplaceable. The earth can create plenty of air, *only if* we maintain the quality of the water, soil, atmosphere, and climate that plants rely on to produce oxygen.

When people say that all life is interconnected, they mean that each organism affects others, and these in turn affect still others. Life forms a complicated web—even minor changes can have unforeseen consequences.

A terrarium can be closed or ventilated. And we have the luxury of changing its conditions to correct for loss of water, overpopulation, or other threats to the system's health. When closed, water circulates through the system as it is drawn up by plant roots, passes through trunks and stems into leaves, and is released as vapor. The vapor condenses into droplets that fall to the ground, where they pass through the soil, losing impurities along the way, and eventually are recaptured by thirsty roots. The plants take carbon dioxide from the air and give off oxygen during the day; at night, they may also release excess carbon dioxide.

A terrarium illustrates both the earth's water cycle and how plants can survive in a balanced, closed system. A terrarium is not only a model for an individual ecosystem, but a symbol of our planet and the need to conserve and preserve its limited resources.

Once you know how to make a terrarium, you can use it to perform experiments testing the effects of

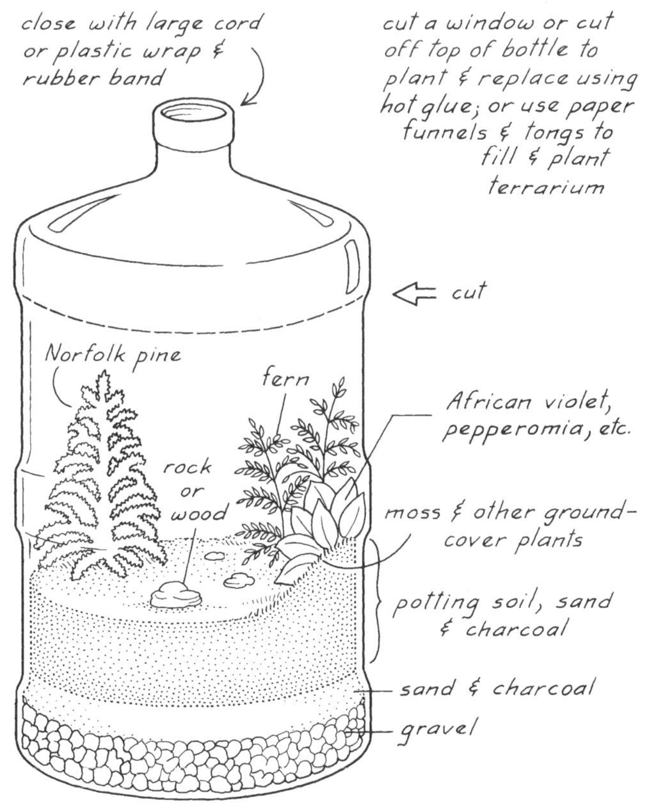

Terrarium made from a plastic, 5-gallon water bottle

This terrarium could also have been planted in an upright position.

poor water quality or set up new ones to simulate other common ecosystems.

STEPS

1. Clean the container and rinse the gravel and charcoal. Decide how to orient your container—some can be planted either on a side or standing upright.
2. Spread a 1-inch layer of gravel in the bottom, and cover it with a ½-inch layer of sand and charcoal. Save some charcoal and sand to mix with your potting soil. These will help filter out impurities in the water and ensure good drainage. Cover the foundation of gravel, sand, and charcoal with about 2 inches of potting soil. Your container should be about a third of the way full now.
3. You may want to sketch out a planting plan before you start, or trace a floor plan of your container and arrange the potted plants on that.
4. To plant, loosen the soil around the roots, make a shallow hole in the soil, and pack the soil firmly around the stem. When planting is complete, water just enough to moisten the soil. Stop if you notice water collecting at the bottom.
5. Close the system with a lid, cover, or clear plastic wrap secured by a rubber band.
6. Put your terrarium in a shady spot for a day or two, then move it to an area that receives plenty of *indirect* light. Too much direct sun will fog up the system and cook the contents.

Beads of water should collect on the sides of the terrarium; if the sides completely fog up, open the container for a few hours to release some of the water. Because your terrarium is not completely closed, you may need to add a little water once in a while, but don't overdo it. Overwatering is more dangerous than underwatering. If you don't notice any beads of water for a week or so, feel the soil. If it's dry, add some water.

Plants for Terrariums

The best terrarium plants are slow-growing and moisture-loving. They also should thrive without direct sunlight. Many tropical plants are well suited to low light levels and high humidity. Ask someone at your local plant store for guidance. Some good choices follow:

Trees and shrubs (for larger terrariums)
Boxwood, Chinese evergreen, dwarf palm, hemlock, Norfolk pine

Ground cover
Creeping charlie, aluminum plant, moss, small-leaved ivy

Plants
African violet, artillery, fittonia, miniature geranium, partridgeberry, pepperomia, prayer, small-leaved philodendron, strawberry begonia, wintergreen

FIND OUT MORE

See Virginie Elbert and George A. Elbert, *Fun with Terrarium Gardening* (New York: Crown Publishers, 1973) (out of print; look for it in your library).

Tips and Tidbits

Different-sized terrarium containers need different amounts of drainage material and soil, but the proportions should remain roughly the same: Fill no more than the bottom fifth of the container with gravel, and cover that with a thin layer of sand and charcoal. Your container should be about a quarter full. Now add soil until the container is about two-fifths full.

The greatest challenge to setting up a terrarium is balancing the water level. Too much, and the vegetation will rot; too little, and it will dry out.

A recycled terrarium can be made from a clear plastic, 2-liter soda bottle (the ones with the black base). Remove the base and plug the holes with tape or hot glue. Fill the base nearly to the top with proportional amounts of charcoal, gravel, and soil, and add plants and water. Cut off the funnel-shaped top (a few inches below the spout), wash it, and turn the cylinder upside down to close the terrarium. Use tape or hot glue to seal it.

A large, plastic, wide-mouthed pretzel barrel or pickle jar also makes a good terrarium.

PLANT A BUTTERFLY AND CATERPILLAR GARDEN

LEVEL: Naturalist (medium; 2 hours)

SEASONS: Spring and summer

MATERIALS:
Plants to attract both butterflies and caterpillars (see listed suggestions)
Small garden plot
Shovel and other planting tools

OPTIONAL
Butterfly guidebook
Stones or logs
Slow-drip water source (water bucket with small hole)

INTRODUCTION

Butterflies are among many insects that go through a complete change in form (metamorphosis). Hatching from an egg, the caterpillar (larva) of a butterfly looks nothing like the delicate, winged creature it will become. In fact, caterpillars look more like dry worms or slugs with feet.

After storing plenty of fat, butterfly caterpillars make a hard-skin chrysalis (from the Greek word meaning "gold") and go into a resting state, called a pupa. During this period, which varies in length among different species, the entire body becomes liquid as tissues and organs are reorganized. Wings, antennae, and six-jointed legs form.

Eventually, a butterfly emerges with crumpled, stunted-looking wings that gradually unfold, dry, and expand, allowing the adult to fly away and begin

Tiger swallowtail butterfly on flower

its mission of feeding, finding a mate, and reproducing.

Many butterflies and caterpillars will visit or eat only very specific kinds of plants. By growing the right plants, you will increase the chances of attracting these insects to your garden. This activity will make it easier to observe the caterpillar's life cycle in later activities.

To attract butterflies to your garden, plant foods for both caterpillars and adults. Each has different needs, so you need both host plants, which the caterpillars eat, and nectar flowers, from which the butterflies drink.

STEPS

1. Before you plant, find out what kinds of butterflies inhabit your area, decide which ones you'd like to attract, and learn what plants attract these species. A guidebook will help you identify the butterflies that share your space. Some field guides list host plants for specific species, and many gardening books include tips for butterfly gardens.

   If you want to attract monarchs and queen butterflies, plant milkweed. Black swallowtails insist on parsley, dill, carrot, Queen Anne's lace, lovage, cow parsnip, or fennel. Sulphur butterflies prefer red clover and alfalfa. Painted ladies love borage, hollyhock, mallows, pearly everlasting, and thistle, the last of which may also attract the monarch-imitating viceroys.
2. Choose a good place to dig a butterfly garden, which should be at least 6 × 6 feet. Because butterflies need sunlight to fly, dig the garden where the plants will receive full sun.
3. Plant a cornucopia of closely packed flowers and herbs. Favor bright colors, especially reds, pinks, oranges, yellows, purples, and lavenders. Avoid using any chemical pesticides if you want butterflies to favor you with their presence.

   In addition to the plants mentioned above, the following flowers are proven butterfly lures: aster, bee balm, bergamot, bleeding heart, cardinal flower, clarkia, columbine, coral bell, cosmos, daisy, dame's rocket, impatiens, lantana, live-forever, marigold, nasturtium, nicotiana (flowering tobacco), petunia, phlox, primrose, rock rose, snapdragon, sweet william, violet, and zinnia. Wisteria vine, honeysuckle, and periwinkle are also popular, as are wildflowers, such as coneflower, goldenrod, ironweed, and verbena. Herbs you should plant are catnip, hyssop, spearmint, and sage.
4. Many bushes and trees are also favorite butterfly or caterpillar hangouts. Plant these in the

Flowers for butterfly gardening include black-eyed susan.

Black swallowtail caterpillar preparing for metamorphosis

backyard to lead butterflies toward their special garden plot. Some favorite butterfly trees and shrubs include autumn olive, azalea, butterfly bush (buddleia), cherry, cotoneaster, cottonwood, dogwood, elderberry, elm, lilac, New Jersey tea, papaw, pear, plum, poplar, privet, rhododendron, tulip, and willow.

Caterpillars feed on many of the above species. Other foods include anise, lupine, and sunflower.

5. To complete your butterfly garden, add large basking rocks or logs, a slow-drip water source, and bits of fruit for the butterflies to snack on.

Find Out More

The NWF publishes a one-page sheet, "Attracting Butterflies to Your Backyard Wildlife Habitat." It's free with self-addressed, stamped envelope, if you write to the address on page 6. See also Mathew Tekulsky, *The Butterfly Garden* (Boston: Harvard Common Press, 1985); and The Xerces Society and the Smithsonian Institution, *Butterfly Gardening* (San Francisco: Sierra Club Books; and Vienna, VA: National Wildlife Federation, 1990).

See also the **Resources** listing, page 123.

Tips and Tidbits

Most caterpillars found in spring and early summer will metamorphose before winter; most found in late summer and fall won't do so until the following spring.

Because butterflies have a low tolerance for pesticides, and many species will reproduce only if particular plants are available, they are considered indicator species. That is, a loss or lack of butterflies often is one of the first signs of an unhealthy environment or one that has deteriorated.

Unlike most insects, butterflies can see red, and they are particularly attracted to flowers of this color.

Child with butterfly

Grow a Live Tepee

LEVEL: Naturalist (medium; 2 hours)

SEASONS: Spring

MATERIALS:

6–8 poles (bamboo, 1" × 2" furring strips, or saplings) at least 6' tall
Strong cord, string, or wire
Shovel
4–6 pole-bean seeds per pole
Bone meal (fertilizer)

OPTIONAL

Legume (bean) inoculant and a jar

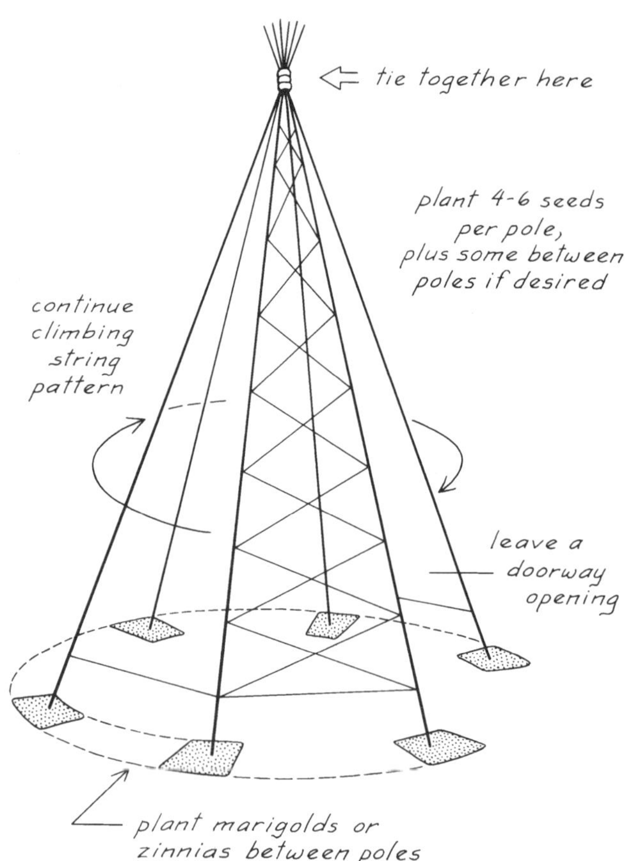

Live tepee, or pole-bean tepee

Digging and adding compost to the planting areas of a live tepee

INTRODUCTION

Most kids love to make a private place of their own, and what better hideaway than a living tepee? This will not only provide youngsters with a secret retreat that they helped build, but their greenhouse also will produce beans to harvest and delicate flowers to enjoy. Some of these flowers will help attract wildlife to your backyard habitat.

STEPS

1. Use sticks or stakes to mark holes in the form of a circle 4 to 6 feet in diameter.
2. Dig a cubic-foot-sized hole for each pole.
3. Prepare the soil by mixing in compost and a teaspoon of bone meal.
4. With the poles lying on their sides, tie the string tightly to one pole, about 6 inches from the top, then loop it around the other poles and tie them into a bundle. Stand the poles up and spread the lower legs until they cover a circle about 6 feet in diameter. This should make the cord at the top taut. If not, tie it with another piece of cord, or get more helpers. Plant the base of each pole firmly into the holes you dug.
5. Tie a climbing string from pole to pole in a

zigzag pattern, starting about 6 inches from the ground on one pole and tying it about halfway up the length of the next pole. Leave the space between two poles open for a doorway (preferably on the tepee's shady north side). With another long piece of string, repeat the zigzag pattern, creating X's between the poles until you reach the doorway again. Climbing string can also run parallel to the ground or in a spiral, with the strands tied about a foot apart on the poles.

6. Prepare to plant, following the directions on the seed package. For best results, inoculate bean seeds by moistening them in a jar, pouring off excess water, and powdering the beans with nitrogen-fixing bacteria. This will help the beans grow strong and produce an abundant harvest.
7. Plant beans around the poles about an inch deep and water them well. The beans should sprout in a week or so. Keep weeds down and help the beans find their climbing strings. At harvest time, eat the beans raw (except scarlet pole beans, which are pretty tough) or cooked, or let them dry on the vine, turning them into wind rattle/chimes or musical instruments.

Find Out More

See Bibby Moore, *Growing with Gardening: A Twelve-Month Guide for Therapy, Recreation, and Education* (Chapel Hill: University of North Carolina Press, 1989). To order, call the publishers at 919-966-3561.

Shelter and shade inside a live tepee

Tips and Tidbits

Beans belong to one of the largest families of flowering plants, the legumes, which include alfalfa, clovers, and peanuts. Legumes take nitrogen from the air and restore the soil's nitrates, nitrogen compounds that are necessary for good plant growth. That's why these and other nitrogen-fixers are sometimes called green manure.

Know your beans: Kentucky wonder and Romano are fast growers; scarlet runner can grow taller than 10 feet, and its red flowers attract hummingbirds.

Grow Some Gourds

LEVEL: Pathfinder (low; 1 hour)

SEASONS: Spring

MATERIALS:

Bottle gourd seeds (*Lagenaria siceraria*)
Shovel
Compost or manure
Trellis, wall, or tepee for climbing
Rubbing alcohol or solution of 1 part chlorine bleach to 10 parts water (for drying)

INTRODUCTION

There are many different kinds of gourds, but among the most popular are calabashes and bottle gourds, also known as dipper, trumpet, or birdhouse gourds. These hard-shelled gourds are popular because you can make many useful and artistic objects from them, including canteens, musical instruments, scoops, ladles, bowls, and, of course, birdhouses and feeders (see the Birdhouse entry on page 124 in the **Resources** listings). You can even cook and eat them, but only when they are very small (they taste like zucchini).

Because of their fast growth, these plants come close to offering first-time gardeners an instant return on their investment of time and energy. They also offer cover for wildlife and sweet-smelling flowers for insects to pollinate.

STEPS

1. Select a planting site. Gourds do best if they have a place to climb, such as a wall, trellis, or tepee (see previous activity). Otherwise, they can overtake your entire lawn. Bottle gourds can be grown anywhere the growing season is at least 130 days, but they grow best in southern climates (where the growing season is long).
2. Read the seed package and follow the directions, which should include soaking the seeds overnight before planting. Seeds can be started indoors, then transplanted outdoors when nighttime temperatures are staying above 55°F.
3. Plant the seeds outdoors about an inch and a half deep and at least a foot apart, in soil enriched with plenty of compost or manure.
4. As the gourds grow, you can write your name or draw a design in them using a nail. Tie elastic bands or cloth to young gourds to make odd shapes as they grow.
5. When the first frost hits, and the stem has turned brown, pick the gourds, leaving several inches of stem attached. To reduce discoloration, wipe gourds with rubbing alcohol or wash them with a solution of 1 part chlorine bleach to 10 parts water.
6. Gourds are 90 percent water, and they have to go through a molding process to dry. This can be done several ways. Some people hang them by the stem. Other people lay them on newspaper or in boxes and turn them once a month. Whichever method you use, choose a cool, dry, airy place (your basement or shaded patio, for instance) to dry them. Be patient, because drying takes anywhere from two weeks for small

Evening-blooming gourd flower

ones to several months for larger ones. When they are hard (and the seeds rattle inside), soak them in warm water, and wash them with dish detergent and a scrub brush to remove the outer skin. When the gourds are dry, they're ready to be worked on.

7. Gourds can be fashioned into hats, handbags, and sculptures. They can be dyed, painted, carved, or decorated with a wood-burning tool. You can also preserve them with a coat of polyurethane or simply polish with floor or car wax and use as decorations. For gourd craft ideas, see the book below.

FIND OUT MORE

See Rita Kohn, *Spring Planting* (Danbury, CT: Children's Press/Grolier, 1995) (for preschool and primary school levels).

See also the **Resources** listing, page 124.

Tips and Tidbits

In India, stringed instruments called sitars, resembling oversized guitars, are made of gourds.

Gourd vines can grow a foot a day and reach 30 feet long.

To encourage large-gourd growth, cut some of the smaller ones off early, so the vine will put more energy into growing the remaining gourds.

BUILD A FLOWER BOX

LEVEL: Naturalist (medium; 3 hours)

SEASONS: Late winter and spring

MATERIALS:

WOOD (pine is good)
1" × 6" × 38"
1" × 4" × 85"
HARDWARE
(40) 1½" #6 flathead wood screws
(4–6) 2" #8 flathead wood screws, or hanging bracket with screws (6d finishing nails may be substituted)
Saw
Drill with #6 and #8 screw countersink bits
Large bit (¼"–½") for drainage holes
Screwdriver (or hammer)
Wood rasp
Sandpaper
Paint or stain

OPTIONAL
Clamps
Plastic window screen

INTRODUCTION

A flower box is a great way to increase your gardening space and brighten the view around your house. Flower boxes are easy to make, and they can be hung outside your child's window or placed on a porch wall, creating a private little garden. A flower box can even serve as a miniature butterfly garden (see activity on page 23). Sow seeds in it, or transplant either store-bought seedlings or those you've started indoors.

STEPS

1. For a window box, measure the window width at the sill—that will be the length of the box. If the window is wider than about 40 inches, consider making two smaller boxes; otherwise, the box will be very heavy when filled with soil, plants, and water.
2. Buy enough wood for a base, front, back, and two sides. This model is 38 inches long and fairly narrow and shallow. You can use 1 × 6-inch wood for the sides as well, making a deeper box (if so, redesign it so the bottom fits *inside*

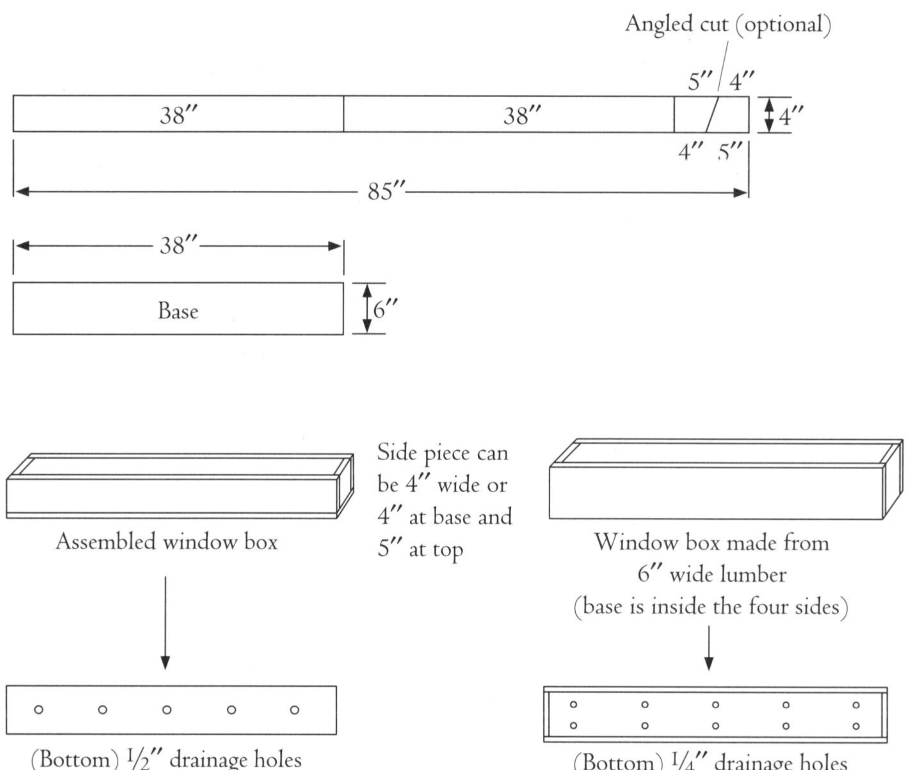

Plans for a small window box

the four sides). If you decide to make a larger box, don't get carried away, because that will increase the challenges of safe, secure mounting. Remember that adding water can triple the weight of the soil.

3. Cut the front, back, and bottom, each 38 inches long. The sides will need to fit between the front and back, so their length is the same as the width of the base (5½ inches), minus 1½ inches (the boards are ¾ inch wide), or 4 inches.
4. Assemble the pieces to check the fit, and clamp them together, if possible. Drill pilot holes into the base and drive in screws. To discourage warping, drive about 12 screws each for the front and back sections, and two for each side. To connect the sides to the front and back, drill two or three pilot holes at each corner connection, and drive in the screws. Sand the edges to eliminate splinters.
5. Turn the assembled box upside down and drill five drainage holes, each about 7 inches apart. If you use a ¼-inch bit, drill two rows of at least five holes each. If you drill ½-inch drainage holes, cut a piece of screen to fit in the bottom (or cover them with pot shards), to prevent soil from escaping. Plastic screen is best; metal screen can be used, but you should paint it to inhibit rust.
6. For protection against rot and warping, paint or stain your box, inside and out. Choose an outdoor-quality wood stain or paint, and select a color that matches or complements either the house main color or trim. Use an old toothbrush to paint inside large drainage holes.
7. Attach the box directly to the windowsill with 2-inch #8 screws. If your windowsill juts out from the side of the house, install a piece of wood between the box and the wall. Depending on how you hang the box, you may want to wait and plant it after it is securely attached to the windowsill.
8. Before planting, add a thin layer of gravel or pot shards on the bottom. Use sterile potting soil, which is lighter than garden soil.

Small flower boxes must be watered about every other day.

When choosing plants to put in your box, consider their needs. Sun-loving flowers won't thrive on the north side of the house, while shade-loving plants will wither under days of full sun. Shade lovers include begonias, impatiens, primrose, and fuchsia; sun lovers include pansies, marigolds, petunias, zinnias, daisies, and chrysanthemums. Many herbs and foliage plants can be grown in flower boxes as well. Because they grow quickly, annuals are probably best for flower boxes. Annuals die at the end of the growing season.

Extend the life of your box by removing it in the late fall and storing it during winter. This is also a good time to give the box a fresh coat of paint or stain, if needed, and change the soil. Put the old soil on the compost pile.

Find Out More

See Kevin McGuire, *Woodworking for Kids: 40 Fabulous, Fun & Useful Things for Kids to Make* (New York: Sterling Publishing Co., 1993); and David Joyce, *Windowbox Gardening* (Old Saybrook, CT: Globe Pequot Press, 1993).

Tips and Tidbits

If you decide to put your flower box on a flat surface (a low wall or stairs, for instance) use some scrap wood to raise it at least a half-inch to allow for drainage and air circulation.

If your box is small, in direct sun, or in a rain-protected location, you will have to water it every other day in summer; if it receives much direct rain, you may need to sprinkle gravel on top to reduce soil loss. Most shaded boxes will need water only twice a week.

Don't water or fertilize your window box plants while they are in direct sunlight; wait until late afternoon or early evening.

Unmounted flower boxes should be raised a few inches above the surface for drainage and air circulation.

PART II

Backyard Residents

Winged Wonders

Make a Nesting Platform

LEVEL: Pathfinder (low; ½ hour)

SEASONS: Winter and early spring

MATERIALS:

WOOD

1" × 8" (actual size ¾" × 7¼") × 22" (pine or exterior-grade plywood is ideal; do not use pressure-treated lumber, which is green colored and contains arsenic)

HARDWARE

(6) 1½" galvanized steel finishing nails (or screws)

(2) large (8d) galvanized steel nails (or screws) for hanging

Square

Saw

Hammer or screwdriver

Drill with ¼" and ⅛" bits

Medium sandpaper and sanding block, or wood rasp

INTRODUCTION

Birds are among the easiest animals to entice to your backyard. With feeders, you can even lure some of them right to your window. But feeders aren't the only way to make your backyard birds feel welcome.

Besides food, birds need shelter for raising young. Different kinds of birds have different nesting needs, so learn about the kinds of birds you want to attract. It won't do any good to build a birdhouse for mockingbirds or goldfinches—they don't like to nest in cavities, whether natural or man-made. Only cavity-dwelling birds—including wrens, woodpeckers, and bluebirds—will use a birdhouse.

Mockingbirds, goldfinches, robins, and phoebes are open-cup nesters, preferring to build their cup-shaped nests in bushes, shrubs, and trees, for the most part. Other birds nest on the ground, and a few build underground nests.

Provide a foundation for some open-cup nesting birds by making nesting platforms. This simple model is a great scrap-lumber project, because it doesn't require much wood, and the design can be easily adapted for the wood you have on hand. You also don't need many tools.

Before you start, though, make sure you have a place to mount the finished platform. Try to find a spot where cats and other predators can't get to it, but where you can see it. After all, one advantage to an open platform is that you can observe the nesting process.

STEPS

The most important part of a nest platform is the base. Its dimensions should be roughly 7 × 7 inches, and it should have drainage holes. The base can be 6 × 8 inches, or even as narrow as 5 × 9 inches. The model described here calls for 1 × 8-inch wood for the base, back, and side.

1. Cut two 7-inch-long pieces for the base and back.
2. Cut an 8-inch-long piece for the side.

3. Assemble these so that the grain of the side and back pieces runs horizontally. If you use screws to put these together, drill pilot holes (just narrower than the thread width) to prevent the wood from splitting.
4. Drill two ¼-inch drainage holes in the base and two ⅛-inch hanging holes near the top of the back.
5. Use a sanding block or wood rasp to round the edges.

   It's not necessary to paint or stain your platform. In fact, the chemicals in wood stain might do more harm than good, so let the platform weather naturally. If you want to darken and protect the wood, coat it with boiled linseed oil and allow it to dry several days before setting it out.
6. Using nails or screws, hang the platform 6 to 15 feet above ground. Because this model has no roof, mount it under an overhang or in an open barn or shed, where it will be protected from rain. If possible, place it so the open sides face away from prevailing winds; southern, eastern, or southeastern exposure is best. Most open-cup-nesting birds are territorial, so don't mount more than two or three platforms per half-acre.

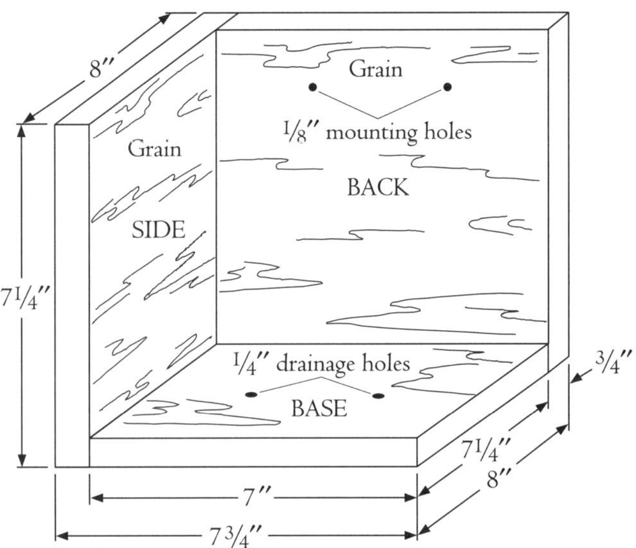

Plans for a nesting platform

Pole-mounted nesting platform surrounded by Virginia creeper vine

Roofed Platform

If you make a second platform, try a slightly more elaborate design. Nail or glue a strip of wood (molding, for example) to the two exposed edges of the base, creating a raised lip that reduces the chance of wind blowing the nest away. Add a one-piece roof, or add another side and a two-piece, A-shaped roof. If you use a one-piece roof, the tops of the sides should be angled, so that the roof slopes and will shed water. The roof should also extend a few inches over the base.

Find Out More

See Len Eiserer, *The American Robin: A Backyard Institution* (Chicago: Nelson-Hall, 1976).

Tips and Tidbits

Robins, which are related to cavity-dwelling bluebirds, nest throughout the United States and Canada. They build nests of twigs, mud, and grass and usually lay three to six sky-blue eggs that hatch after about two weeks. Robins often raise two families per season, and some pairs even manage to raise three. Three states have chosen the robin as their official state bird: Connecticut, Michigan, and Wisconsin.

If a nest remains at the end of winter, remove it, because most birds won't reuse an old nest.

Help your local robins, swallows, and other mud-nest builders by creating a small mud puddle in your yard. You may want to rig up a bucket or barrel with a small hole in the bottom as a slow-leak water supply. Avoid creating stagnant puddles of water that could attract breeding mosquitos.

BUILD A BIRDHOUSE

LEVEL: Naturalist (medium; 1–2 hours)

SEASONS: Winter, early spring, and even fall (birds may use it as a roost)

MATERIALS:

WOOD

1" × 6" (actual size ¾" × 5½") × 47½" long (pine, exterior-grade plywood, or cedar are ideal; do not use pressure-treated lumber, which is greenish and contains arsenic)

HARDWARE

Square

Saw

1½", 4d galvanized steel finishing nails (or #6 wood screws); large, galvanized steel nails for hanging (or screws) (for best hold, use either screws or ring-shank nails)

Hammer (or screwdriver)

Drill with entrance-hole-sized bit (1⅛"–1½")

¼" bit for ventilation and drainage holes (also 1⁄16" bit, if needed for pilot holes)

Medium sandpaper and a sanding block or wood rasp

OPTIONAL

Short piece of wood molding or weatherproof caulking

INTRODUCTION

More than 80 species of North American birds are cavity nesters. They include several kinds of ducks and owls, kestrels, woodpeckers, flickers, sapsuckers, flycatchers, wrens, chickadees, nuthatches, titmice, and bluebirds. Roughly half of these cavity nesters commonly use birdhouses, and most of them are efficient and voracious insect eaters.

Just about every building and road we construct eliminates trees, which cavity nesters use. By building and putting up birdhouses, you decrease the competition among birds for safe and secure nest cavities.

Check the previous activity for tips on wood finishes.

STEPS

(The following one-board plan is adapted from *Woodworking for Wildlife;* see **Find Out More.**)

1. Choose a 1 × 6-inch board that is as free from flaws as possible.
2. Use a square to mark the cuts as follows: 11 inches (back), 8 inches (three pieces: front, and the two sides), 8¼ inches (roof), and 4 inches (bottom). (If you are using ⅞-inch boards, such as cedar, the bottom should be 3⅞ inches.) Make your cut marks thick enough to accommodate the width of the saw blade.
3. Cut the pieces. If there is a rough side—as with cedar—use it on the outside.
4. Drill a hole in the front, an inch from the top

Entrance-Hole Sizes

Different sources list different-sized entrance holes for the same species. To exclude house sparrows, the hole diameter must be less than 1¼ inches; to exclude starlings, it must be 1½ inches or smaller. A hole of 1⅛ inches is good for accommodating wrens and chickadees; 1¼ inches for nuthatches and other small birds; and up to 1½ inches for most other common backyard cavity-nesters.

5. Drill ¼-inch ventilation and drainage holes: two at the top of each side and four in the floor.
6. Drill pilot holes ¼ inch from the top and bottom of the back for easier hanging. If you are using a wood such as cedar, drill pilot holes for nails or screws to help prevent it from splitting. This is often advisable, especially if small hands will be driving the nails.
7. Fasten the left side midway between the top and bottom of the back board.
8. Fasten the floor piece ¼ inch above the bottom edge of the side board to reduce moisture seepage and rot.
9. Fasten the front to the side and bottom. Attach the roof.
10. The right side requires special attention, since it will be a swinging door, to allow for cleaning. Draw a line on the right edge of the front and back, about 1½ inches down from the roof. These are your pivot-nail marks, so the side opens for easy cleaning.
11. Place the right side, leaving ⅛ inch between the roof and the top of the side, to allow the side to swing open.
12. Fasten the right side with two top nails.
13. Drill a latch hole on the lower right side of the front.
14. Either drive the nail partway in or use a slightly smaller nail to hold the side closed.
15. Check that the side door opens and be sure no sharp nails or splinters protrude inside that could hurt the tenants.
16. Using a sanding block or wood rasp, smooth the edges.
17. If you have a scrap piece of quarter-round molding, nail it where the roof and back meet at the top to reduce rain seepage. Alternatively, apply weatherproof caulking along the seam.
18. Mount your birdhouse to a pole, post, or tree, at least 5 feet from the ground and within reach, so

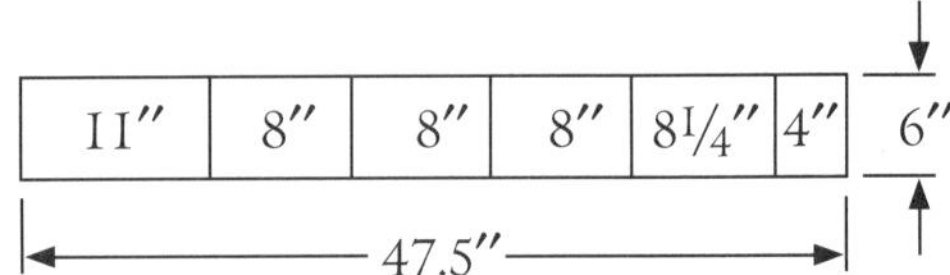

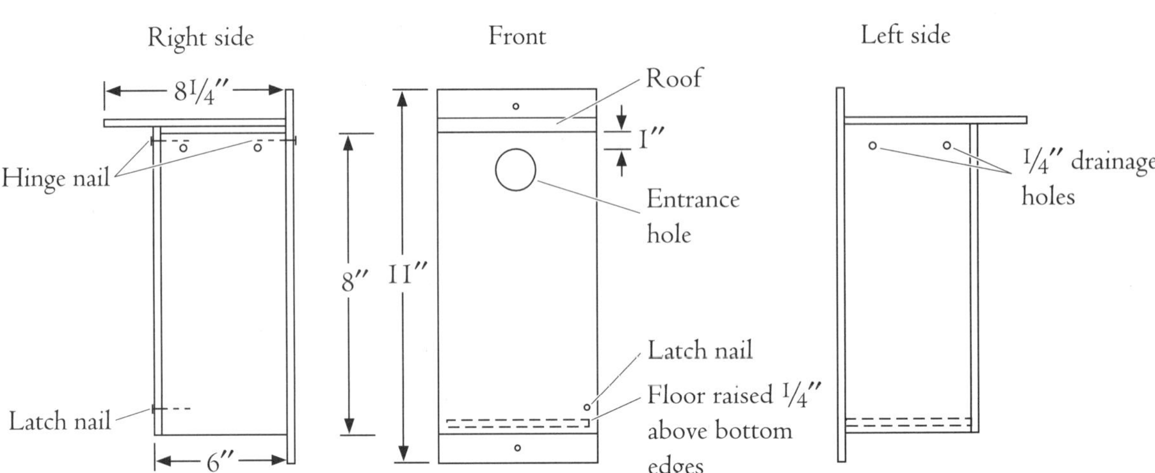

One-board plan for a birdhouse

you can clean it. Try to find a spot where you can watch the comings and goings of its residents.

Long Term

Clean out your nesting box at the end of each season and check it again in late winter or early spring. Don't be surprised if a mouse has built its nest in your vacant winter cottage. Mice may kill returning songbirds in the spring, so some people plug birdhouse holes in wintertime or leave one side open.

Find Out More

See Carrol L. Henderson, *Woodworking for Wildlife,* 2nd ed. (St. Paul: Minnesota Department of Natural Resources, 1992). Call Minnesota's Bookstore at 800-657-3757, or write them at 117 University Ave., St. Paul MN 55155. Also, Donald Stokes and Lillian Stokes, *The Complete Birdhouse Book: The Easy Guide to Attracting Nesting Birds* (New York: Little, Brown and Co., 1990).

See also the **Resources** listing, page 124.

Tips and Tidbits

Perches on birdhouses do more harm than good. Only a few bird species, such as house sparrows and starlings, appreciate them, and some predators find them convenient. But the birds you want to attract will get along better without a perch.

When mounting your bird box, remember who it's for and what habitat they like. Bluebirds like wide, open spaces; wrens like a mixture of open areas, trees, shrubs, and brush piles. Also, pay attention to territory requirements. Chickadee pairs generally won't let other chickadees within about a 100-yard radius; wrens may tolerate other wrens, if they stay at least 35 yards away.

There's no harm in putting up birdhouses in the fall. Birds that stay in your area during winter may use them for night roosts. Some people even build special winter-roosting boxes.

Build a Bird Nest

LEVEL: Pathfinder (low; 1 hour)

SEASONS: Late winter and spring

MATERIALS:
Twigs, grass, leaves, mud, feathers, thread, etc.

Introduction

Birds build nests using many different materials. Robins use mud, grass, and sticks. Wrens may use thread, fluff from milkweed, grasses, and twigs. Swallows just use mud. Some birds build their nests out of pebbles or lay their eggs on a ledge. Young birds often build sloppier nests than older, more experienced birds, but even beginners build better nests than most humans can. Try to match the birds at their craft.

Steps

1. Look for nests in your neighborhood and—without disturbing them—study the building materials and how they are assembled. If you can't find any nests, look for pictures in bird books or magazines.
2. Gather outdoor nesting materials. You can also use cotton balls, hair, and thread from indoors. Then find an outdoor spot where you and your kids can make a mess.
3. Working separately or together, build a nest as much like a bird's as possible. It's harder than you might think, but then, most birds spend a week or more at the task. One of the easiest nests to build is the robin's. Start with mud and larger sticks to make a foundation, adding smaller sticks and mud to build walls. As the mud dries, line

Making a homemade nest is no simple task for humans.

the inside with twigs and grasses, finishing with soft bits of fluff to protect and insulate the eggs.

When you're finished, compare your building project with a bird's. Who's the master builder? Afterward, put your nest in the branches of a tree where birds can "borrow" your materials for their nests.

FIND OUT MORE

See Rebecca Rupp, *Everything You Never Learned About Birds: Lore & Legends, Science & Nature Hands-On Projects* (Pownal, VT: Storey Communications, 1995); and Hal H. Harrison, *A Field Guide to Birds' Nests* (Boston: Houghton Mifflin Co., 1975).

Tips and Tidbits

Hummingbird nests (usually made of lichens, spiderwebs, and plant parts) are roughly walnut-sized.

Belted kingfishers nest in tunnels, laying their eggs in the sand or on regurgitated fish bones. Baltimore orioles weave intricate nests that hang from tree branches like inflated pockets. Coots, grebes, and some other birds nest on mounds of vegetation that float on water.

Bald eagles build the biggest nests, made of sticks and other materials, that measure up to 10 feet across and 10 feet deep. Eagles often return to the same breeding grounds during their 20-year life span, so their nests can grow to weigh hundreds or even thousands of pounds, heavy enough to topple a host tree.

Nest building for many birds may take a week and require more than a hundred material-gathering trips. Woodpeckers may take several weeks to hollow out a cavity.

Cowbirds don't build nests. They lay their eggs in the nests of other birds—often evicting the owner's eggs—and let the original nest owner incubate and raise the cowbird's young.

BUILD A BIRD FEEDER

LEVEL: Naturalist (medium; 1 hour)

SEASONS: Fall and winter

MATERIALS:

WOOD

1" × 10" pine or a 1" × 10" × 15" piece of exterior-grade plywood (measurements can vary widely)

1" × ½" or 1½" × ½" molding (can vary)

HARDWARE

Small, 1" brads (or exterior glue)

(2–3) 2" nails or screws

Hammer or screwdriver

OPTIONAL

Small nails, hooks, or eyelet screws

Drill and bit (for drilling mounting pilot holes)

INTRODUCTION

A simple feeding platform can be built with a minimum of materials, possibly even scavenged from your scrap-lumber pile or that of a neighbor or local woodworker. As with the nesting platform described on page 35 the dimensions of your feeding platform can vary widely, depending on your needs and wood supply.

This is a good midlevel feeder, but it can also be mounted on a windowsill near the ground or higher up. One of the beauties of this design is its dual purpose: seeds will fall through drainage gaps, so you'll automatically be feeding birds at two levels. Mounted on a windowsill, it is probably the easiest feeder to keep stocked and clean.

Gray squirrel at platform feeder

STEPS

1. Decide on a location for your feeding platform. This can be on a stump, a fence post, a fairly straight limb, a windowsill, or any other workable spot. If you plan to mount the platform on a windowsill, make it about the same width as the window.
2. Nail or glue strips of wood on the top surface of the platform or around the edges. Leave ½-inch gaps at the corners or drill a dozen ⅛-inch holes in the base to allow water to drain off.
3. Add small nails, hooks, or eyelet screws around the edges or underneath for hanging mesh bags filled with suet or nesting materials.
4. Mount to a windowsill with screws or nails driven straight into the sill. If your platform extends very far, you may want to attach support brackets underneath. Alternatively, mount with screws or nails to a wooden post, a four-by-four, or a stump (a foot off the ground is adequate; several feet off the ground will provide more protection from predators). Posts should be planted firmly in the ground, at least 2 feet deep. You can also attach four short legs (about a foot long) to the platform and set it out in the yard. The only problem with putting

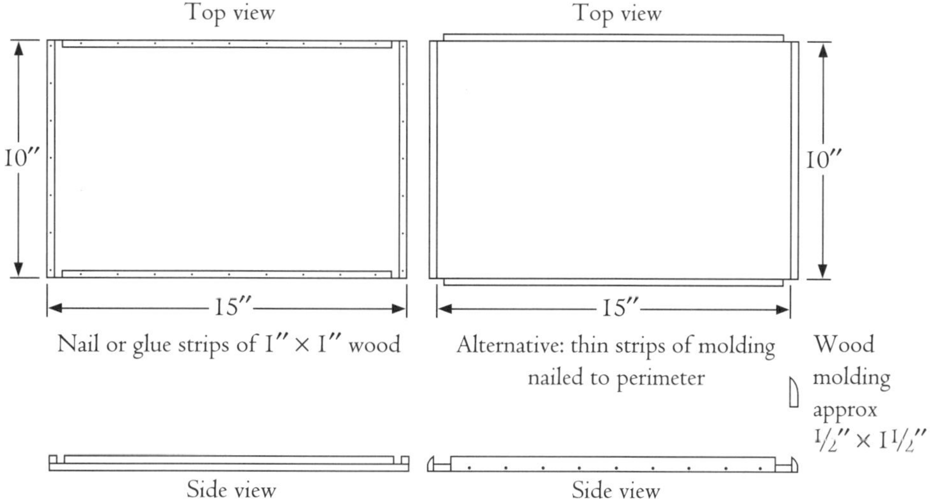

Plan for a platform feeder (top and side views)

your platform feeder out in the open is that the wind may blow the seeds away.

Because this feeder has no roof, be sparing with the seed. Put out only about as much as the birds are likely to eat in a day. Otherwise, even with drainage, some seed will probably rot. Also, if you drilled holes for drainage, keep a length of coat hanger wire handy to poke out stuck seeds. Use an old spatula or hairbrush to free the feeder of old seeds that get stuck along the edges. If the feeder gets very dirty, scrub it with a solution of 2 ounces of bleach mixed with a gallon of water and let it dry thoroughly.

Find Out More

See "Birds, Birds, Birds," in *Ranger Rick's NatureScope* (Vienna, VA: National Wildlife Federation, 1992).

See also the **Resources** listing, page 124.

Mourning doves prefer to feed on the ground or from a platform.

Tips and Tidbits

Crushed eggshells are an excellent source of calcium for egg-laying females. Mix some in with your seeds in early spring.

Don't let sunflower shells collect around plants, and don't put them in your compost pile. Not only do they contain a poison (possibly the result of oil in the shells that turns rancid) that will kill plants, but they may encourage the growth of harmful molds.

Create a Wild-Bird Diorama

LEVEL: Naturalist (medium; 1 hour)

SEASONS: Fall and winter

MATERIALS:
Bird feeders
Birdseed and suet

Introduction

Every year more than 60 million people feed backyard birds. That's not even counting kids under age 16. On average, one out of three homes in America stocks bird feeders, spending more than $2 billion a year on birdseed.

If you're not yet feeding your winged residents, it's easy to get started. If you're already doing it, you can expand your feeding set-up to satisfy more birds. In addition, you can make your backyard habitat more bird-friendly by planting fruit-, seed-, nut-, and berry-bearing plants (see Gardening for the Birds activities, pages 45–47).

Feeding the birds is not only entertaining and educational for you, it helps them survive in winter, when just a few hours of hunger and chill can mean death.

Steps

1. Buy or make as many feeders as you think your yard can support.

2. Using your backyard habitat map, consider the best places to locate your feeding stations. Don't just randomly distribute individual feeders. Create feeding stations, complete with multilevel feeders and water, if possible.
3. Place feeders at various levels to satisfy the needs of ground-, middle-, and upper-story feeders. Placing raised feeders near cover will help increase their use, because the birds will feel safer. If you notice that few birds visit a particular feeder, try another location. You'll know you're on the right track when your backyard looks like a bustling wild-bird diorama.

Long Term

Once birds grow accustomed to finding food at your house, continue feeding at least through the winter. Brush off snow from your feeders as soon as possible after a storm. Also flatten the snow beneath and around feeders, and spread some seeds for the ground-feeders. Some people continue feeding throughout the year. Although year-round feeding is not harmful, it is unnecessary for most seed-eating birds. Nectar-feeding birds, such as hummingbirds, can be fed in summer; specially designed feeders are made for them.

Find Out More

See John V. Dennis, *The Complete Guide to Bird Feeding* (New York: Alfred A. Knopf, 1996).

See also the Bird Feeder entry in the **Resources** listings, page 124.

Purple finch at homemade feeder

Tips and Tidbits

Chickadees and some other birds will take sunflower seeds from your open hand. It may take a while for them to begin to trust you, but the feeling of a wild bird on your hand is worth the effort.

Instead of tossing salt on your sidewalk to melt snow, use birdseed to improve traction. This saves your soil while providing tidbits for titmice and other frosty feathered friends.

Not all wintertime birds have the same eating habits. Sparrows, towhees, mourning doves, and grosbeaks like to feed on the ground. Finches, chickadees, and others prefer to feed above ground from a perch, making tube feeders especially suitable. Many larger birds, such as cardinals and bluejays, prefer platform feeders, which many ground-level feeders also use. Some birds will feed just about anywhere.

Different seed types attract different bird species. Finches, cardinals, and many other birds like sunflower seeds. Pine siskins, woodpeckers, wrens, and nuthatches love suet. Chickadees and titmice, among others, favor both. Experiment with different foods, including cracked corn, hulled sunflower seeds, cracked and whole peanuts, and other foods.

Make Baths for Birds and Other Critters

LEVEL: Pathfinder (low; ½ hour)

SEASONS: All

MATERIALS:

Unglazed clay saucer (the kind that go under potted plants), 12" to 20" diameter or larger
Spade, or other digging tool (for ground placement)
Stump or a low wall (for raised placement)
Scrub brush
Garden hose with spray nozzle
Bucket (for adding water when the hose is out of use)

INTRODUCTION

Besides food, shelter, and places to raise young, birds need water to survive. Of course, this applies not only to birds, but to most other animals. For many creatures, water becomes most critical in winter, when many supplies may be iced over. Adding a water source to your backyard habitat can greatly increase the number of birds and other animals using your backyard. You may even be able to double the number of wildlife visitors, improving their chances for survival and increasing your wildlife-watching pleasure.

STEPS

1. Find an unglazed, clay saucer. The larger, the better, but it shouldn't be filled more than about 2½ inches deep.
2. Set it in the ground in an open area or near a low tree. The bath should be angled, so there is a shallow wading area and a deep end for bathing. You can also put the bath on a stump or a low garden wall.
3. Plant a limb or other perch in the ground nearby to give birds a chance to survey the situation before they take the plunge.

Long Term

In cold weather, keep the bath free of ice during the day. Also, change the water regularly—daily, if possible. Even better, use a recirculating pump to provide a constant flow of water running in and out. Just the sound of trickling water will often attract some unusual visitors, such as warblers. If the water stands too long, especially in direct sunlight, bacteria grow faster, and your birds may be in danger

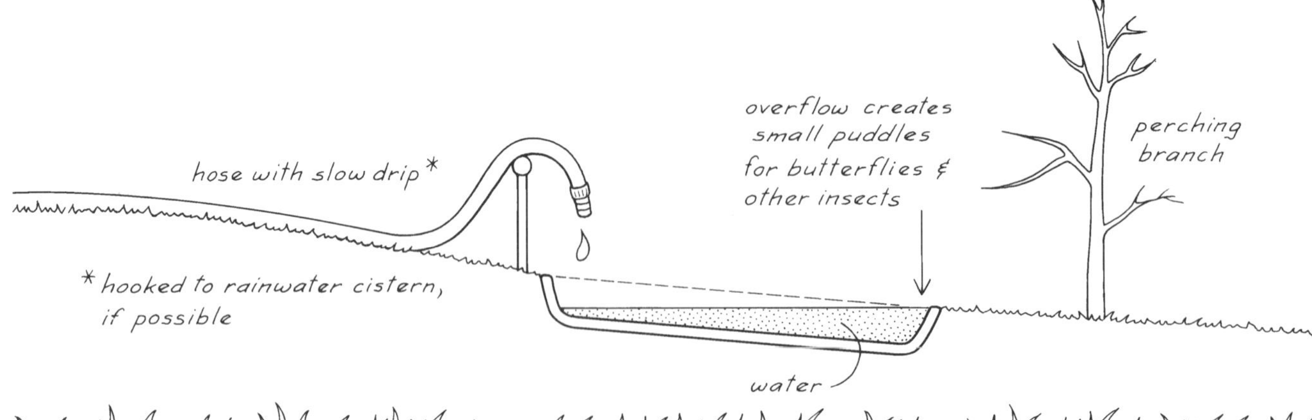

Ground-level birdbath with drip hose

of catching a waterborne disease. Stagnant water also invites mosquitos to breed.

If your birdbath gets grungy, scrub it with a soft brush and water containing 1 teaspoon of chlorine bleach per gallon, then rinse it very well, and let it dry before refilling. A high-pressure spray nozzle will also do the trick. Clean the bath at least once a week during hot weather.

You may find that your bath attracts creatures besides birds, including butterflies, squirrels, raccoons, opossums, and chipmunks, especially if it rests on the ground. Ground-level baths may be dangerous for animals, though, if you have free-ranging cats in your neighborhood. If possible, set up two baths, one raised and one on the ground. Although bells are not always effective, try to get neighborhood cats fitted for sound.

Find Out More

See Noble Proctor, *Garden Birds: How to Attract Birds to Your Garden* (Emmaus, PA: Rodale Press, 1985).

See also the **Resources** listing, page 125.

Squirrel drinking from bath

Tips and Tidbits

Birds—including hummingbirds—also enjoy an occasional shower. Tie your hose to a stake and adjust the spray nozzle at a light, rainlike setting. Put this near a thirsty plant and achieve two purposes—watering the plants and the animals.

Never add salt or other antifreeze or fungicidal chemical additives to your birdbath. By preventing it from freezing and protecting the water from fungus, you may endanger the health of your wildlife visitors.

Hang a bucket with a small hole in the bottom above your bath to create a trickling waterfall that supplies a gradual stream of fresh water splashing into your birdbath.

Some birds enjoy not only wet baths but dry ones. Leave a dry patch for dust baths. These are believed to help birds kill lice and other parasites.

Gardening for the Birds

LEVEL: Explorer (high; several hours)

SEASONS: Spring, summer, and fall

MATERIALS:
Backyard habitat map (see activity on page 3)
Bird-food producing plants (see list below)
Gardening tools

Introduction

Feeding birds store-bought seed is a quick and easy way to attract wildlife, but most of us could be doing more. An excellent long-term activity is gardening for birds: planting trees, bushes, vines, and other bird-food producing plants, which also create more nesting and shelter areas for birds. When you turn your yard into an abundantly stocked, natural-foods co-op for birds, you also improve your backyard habitat for many other animals. You probably already have some food-bearing plants, but almost any yard could offer more.

Gardening for the birds is a great way to learn more about bird needs and habits while improving their habitat. You'll learn which plantings attract birds and which will do well in your region.

STEPS

1. As with any long-term landscaping project, planning is the key to success. You don't want to plant sun-loving bushes in deep shade or shade lovers in full sun. You also don't want to plant a tree where it will be casting its long shadow on your sun-loving bushes and vines in five years. So use your backyard habitat map and look for areas where some food plants could be added. Study your yard to identify areas that get full sun most of the day, and those that receive only partial sun and shade.

   One goal of wildlife gardening is to reduce lawn area and increase wildlife areas. You may want to turn a grassy patch into a natural, low-maintenance bird-refueling station.
2. Once you have identified good planting places, hit the books to discover which plants should be put where. Your choice of plants will depend on your region. Where possible, choose native plants—those that grow naturally in your part of the country. Remember that you want food-bearing plants not only for summer and fall but also for the winter months.

Dogwood trees not only produce beautiful flowers for us to enjoy, but provide nesting places and seeds for birds.

Virginia creeper vine provides thick nesting cover as well as food for birds.

FAVORITE BIRD PLANTINGS

Craig Tufts, Backyard Wildlife Habitat specialist for the National Wildlife Federation, has been gardening for birds and other wildlife for many years. Here is his short list of favorite bird plantings.

TREES

Junipers (a type of cedar), such as eastern red cedar (*Juniperus virginiana*), Rocky Mountain (*J. scopulorum*), common (*J. communis,* which is more shrublike), and Chinese (*J. chinensis;* some varieties are trees and some shrubs). Several hollies, including the Nellie Stevens, American, and Fosteri varieties. Magnolia, flowering dogwood, autumn olive, sassafras, spruce, and hemlock are also excellent food producers.

BUSHES AND SHRUBS

Cotoneasters—some varieties grow as evergreens in

warm climates, and some grow to 15 feet high. Look for these varieties: bearberry (*Cotoneaster dammeri*), cranberry (*C. apiculatus*), and spreading (*C. divaricatus*), among others. Staghorn sumac (*Rhus typhina*), viburnums, and wild roses also are productive.

VINES

Wild grapes, Virginia creeper, and bittersweet.

FLOWERS

Many flowers produce seeds that birds love to eat, with annuals being the most productive. Favorites include sunflowers (and other members of the daisy family), calendula, California poppy, cornflower, cosmos, zinnias, marigolds (except the mule variety), four o'clocks, petunias, St. John's worts, wild aster, garden phlox, coreopsis, and prickly pear cactus (a source of fruit and seeds). Avoid hybrids, most of which are poor food sources. Leave most of the seed-filled flower heads on the plants for birds to eat. Harvest the rest and plant them next year.

GRASSES

Those that provide not only shelter but food include switch grass, broom sedge, and Indian grass.

MISCELLANEOUS

Just about any berry-bearing tree, shrub, vine, or other plant will draw birds. In addition to those mentioned above, try firethorn (*Pyracantha coccinea*), mountain ash (*Sorbus* species), and winterberry holly (*Ilex verticillata*). Wild cherry, mulberry, and flowering crabapple are also favorites.

Some weeds, such as poison ivy, oak, and sumac, crabgrass, and pokeweed also provide food for birds.

Find Out More

See Anne Halpin, *For the Birds! A Handy Guide to Attracting Birds to Your Backyard* (New York: Henry Holt and Co., 1996) (entry-level); and George Adams, *Birdscaping Your Garden* (Emmaus, PA: Rodale Press, 1994).

See also the **Resources** listing, page 125.

Tips and Tidbits

Variety is the key to bird gardening, as with all wildlife gardening. You want many different species of plants, as well as different heights and densities.

Allow leaves to collect under at least some shrubs and trees, so towhees, robins, thrushes, and other ground-scratchers have good insect-hunting grounds.

Gardening for Hummingbirds

LEVEL: Explorer (high; several hours)

SEASONS: Spring and summer

MATERIALS:
Backyard habitat map (see activity on page 3)
Hummingbird plantings (see list below)
Gardening tools

INTRODUCTION

Just about everyone loves hummingbirds. These almost impossibly perfect creations seem too small to be real. In fact, the world's smallest bird is the Cuba's bee hummingbird. It weighs only 1/15 ounce, about the same as a dime. Some hummers flap their wings at 40 to 80 beats a second, and some species can hum along at an astounding rate of more than 150 beats a second. Hummingbirds also are the only birds that can fly backwards.

Despite their charms, hummingbirds can be belligerent. Just sit on a porch surrounded by nectar-bearing flowers or several hummingbird feeders, and close your eyes. You may get the impression that you are in the middle of an aerial war zone, with mega-mosquito-sized bombers buzzing and strafing each other.

Attract hummingbirds to your backyard habitat, and you will enjoy hours of free entertainment as you watch one of nature's most fascinating creations.

STEPS

1. Look at your backyard habitat map (see page 3) for suitable locations. You'll want a sunny spot that has some space around it. The patch should be at least 10 × 10 feet. Ideally, it will be within range of several observation windows or near a patio.
2. Once you have several possible sites in mind, narrow down the possibilities by walking around your yard and envisioning the finished plot.
3. When you have selected a location, mark the area with stakes and/or string and start digging.
4. Add compost to enrich the soil. You may want to include a birdbath or a pole for hanging a hummingbird feeder or two until your garden has become more productive.
5. In choosing plants, consult the list below. Some of the plants that attract hummingbirds also attract birds or butterflies. As much as possible, choose dual-purpose plants, to get the most from each one.

Special feeders also attract hummers. For tips on mixing your own liquid food, see the **Resources** *listing, page 125.*

Top Hummingbird Plants

Most plants with showy, tube-shaped, nectar-bearing flowers—especially those that are bright red, pink, orange, or yellow—will draw hummingbirds to your backyard habitat. The following list includes some plants that bloom early and some that bloom late in summer. Favorite bird and/or butterfly plants are marked with an asterisk.

FLOWERS
*Bee balm, *bergamot, bergena, *butterfly weed, cleome, *columbine (American or European), *coral-bells, delphinium, evening primrose, *four o'clock, foxglove, fuchsia, *geranium, gladiolus, hibiscus, *impatiens (touch-me-not), jewelweed, lilies (especially plantain/hosta), *nasturtium, *nicotiana (flowering tobacco), *petunia, *phlox, salvia (scarlet sage), snap-dragon, *zinnia.

Eastern wildflowers, including *cardinal flower and trumpet creeper (or hybrids). Western wildflowers, including scarlet paintbrush, Pacific Northwest columbine, red-flowering currant, scarlet penstemon. Other western favorites: agave, filias, lobelia, manzanita, monkey flowers, ocotillo, *prickly pear, scarlet passion flower, wild pink, yucca.

VINES
Flame, honeysuckle, morning glory, scarlet runner pole bean.

SHRUBS
Azalea, coralberry, flowering quince, honeysuckle, lilac, rhododendron, weigela.

TREES
Chinaberry, *flowering crabapple, *hawthorn, locust, mimosa, tulip tree. Trees with dense foliage—evergreens, deciduous trees, and shrubs—may entice hummers to nest in your yard.

Find Out More

See Mathew Tekulsky, *The Hummingbird Garden* (New York: Crown Publishers, 1990).

See also the **Resources** listing, page 125.

Tips and Tidbits

Worldwide, there are 320 species of hummingbirds. Of the 15 North American species, only the ruby-throated is commonly found east of the Mississippi River.

On its migration from Central America in winter to North America in spring, the ruby-throated hummingbird may travel 2,000 miles and cross the Gulf of Mexico.

Some hummingbirds can fly up to 60 miles an hour, but they aren't the fastest birds in the sky. One Asian swift can zoom along at nearly 220 miles an hour, and the peregrine falcon attains speeds close to 200 miles an hour.

Spiders, ants, gnats, fruit flies, and other small insects and larvae provide protein for many hummingbirds.

Nineteenth-century naturalist John James Audubon described hummingbirds as a "glittering fragment of the rainbow."

Arthropods

MAKE AN ARTHROPOD CAGE (BUGARIUM)

LEVEL: Naturalist (medium; about 2 hours)

SEASONS: Spring, summer, and fall

MATERIALS:

2 pine boards (can be scrap or thin plywood), ½ to ¾" thick, and at least 3" × 4"

Screen (plastic or metal), about a foot wide and a little longer than the circumference of the end pieces

Thin wood (for door to cover entrance)

Scissors (heavy duty, for cutting screen)

Staple gun (to attach the screen) or thin wood strips and tacks

Drill with ⅛" and 1½" bits (for the large hole, a saw bit works best)

Wood screw, flatheaded, about 1", depending on wood

Wood rasp or sandpaper and sanding block

OPTIONAL

Modeling clay, waterproof glue, or hot glue

Thin strip of wood (⅛" × ¾", ¾" rounded, or ½" × ¾"), long enough to go around all edges, top and bottom

INTRODUCTION

Some people complain about insects, spiders, and other arthropods (joint-legged creatures), but every backyard wildlife habitat has them. Maybe that's because they're so numerous—more than three-fourths of all animals in the world are arthropods. Many are helpful in the garden, and there's really very little we can do about the "bad" ones except learn to live with them. Just about all of them are important foods for birds, snakes, toads, and other wildlife, and many exhibit amazing adaptations for survival.

To observe some of these fascinating and abundant creatures, make a bugarium. You'll find insects, arachnids, and all the others are among the most interesting (and numerous) backyard inhabitants.

STEPS

1. Make two square end-pieces. Size can vary, from a few inches to 10 × 10 inches, or even larger. Minimum size is about 3 × 4 inches. If you want, you can also make a wooden wall (or floor, as the case may be); an advantage of the

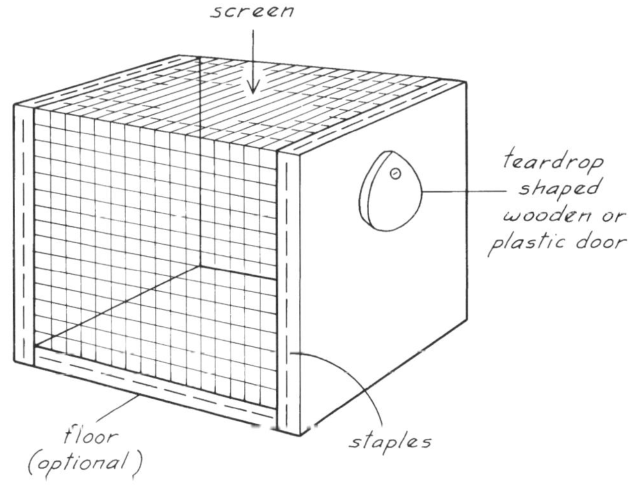

A floor (or wall) adds stability to this small bugarium.

wall/floor is that you don't have to connect the ends of the screen to each other. Also, you have a light-colored surface inside, which makes it easier to see the residents.

2. Cut a hole in one of the end-pieces, roughly in the middle.
3. Place the door over the hole.
4. Drill a ⅛-inch pilot hole through the door and into the side, and drive the screw in so the door slides open easily.
5. Use a wood rasp or sandpaper to round all edges and eliminate splinters.
6. Cut the screen to fit (with about an inch overlap) and staple it to the edges of the base. To ensure a bug-tight container, be generous with the staples. If you don't have a staple gun, use tacks and thin wood strips or cardboard.
7. Fill gaps between screen and base with modeling clay, or with waterproof or hot glue.
8. For the best appearance (and to reduce the number of exposed wire-ends), glue or nail 1 × 1-inch or ⅛ × 1-inch wood around the edges.
9. Use a piece of screen wire (or needle and thread) to sew the overlapping pieces of screen together. Keep the edges aligned, or the top section won't fit properly.
10. Staple the top in place, again filling any gaps. Your bugarium is ready for occupancy. If your bug box has no wall/floor, don't put much pressure on top, or it will collapse.

Super-duper Bug Box

Make a super-duper bug box with two pieces of 8 × 12 × ¾-inch plywood and 32 inches of 12-inch-wide metal screen. Staple base, as above. Cut the 2½-inch hole near the top edge of one side and attach sliding door. On the other edge, use a coping saw to cut a 4 × 5-inch door. Staple the top board in place, minus the hinged door. Glue or nail thin strips of wood (⅛ × 1 inch) along the top of the hinged door to make a bug-proof lip. Glue or nail a strip of 1 × 1-inch wood to the hinged door side and staple the screen to that. Sand or file the inside front edge of the hinged door so it will close properly. Use two small hinges to attach the swing door to the top. For support, cut a piece of 2 × 2-inch wood and glue or screw it in the middle, running from top to bottom. Attach a knob to the door, if desired, and a carrying handle on top in the middle.

Black swallowtail butterfly in cage

Find Out More

See Sally Kneidel, *Pet Bugs: A Kid's Guide to Catching & Keeping Touchable Insects* (New York: John Wiley & Sons, 1994).

Tips and Tidbits

Insects outnumber all other life-forms on Earth. About a million species (different kinds) have been identified, and scientists discover about 1,000 new species every year. There are probably several million more, and possibly as many as 30 million more. That's species, not individuals. The number of individual insects is unknown, but estimates range from half a billion to 400 billion of them crawling, jumping, swimming, and flying around the planet. Other known arthropods number about 500,000 species.

Unless you're sure you can provide for their needs, don't keep your captives more than a day or so. Give them food and water. A wet cotton ball in a bottle cap quenches their thirst. Make their artificial environment as similar to their natural environment as possible.

Keep records of your houseguests. Jot down where you found them, and when they checked in and out. Note what they do at different times of the day.

Make an Arthropod Vacuum and a Pitfall Trap

LEVEL: Pathfinder (low; about ½ hour)

SEASONS: Spring, summer, and fall

MATERIALS:

FOR VACUUM

Flexible straws (the kind you can angle); you may be able to get a suction tube with a filter cap from your dentist

Clear container with lid (can be glass or plastic)

Gauze or nylon stocking (about a square inch)

Small rubber band

Modeling clay, waterproof glue, or hot-glue gun

FOR PITFALL TRAP

2 or more containers (glass, metal, or plastic, should be at least 2" deep)

Heavy cardboard or wooden board (can be scrap; should more than cover the container)

Several small rocks or other props to raise the covering board

Bait (fruits, vegetables, meat, cheese, fresh and old leaves)

OPTIONAL

Magnifying glass

INTRODUCTION

Now that you have an insect cage (see previous activity), you may need equipment with which to collect some inhabitants. An insect vacuum—also known as a pooter or aspirator—will help you gather and observe small animals that you prefer not to touch. The pitfall trap will help you to catch beetles and other larger critters and to experiment with different foods as insect lures.

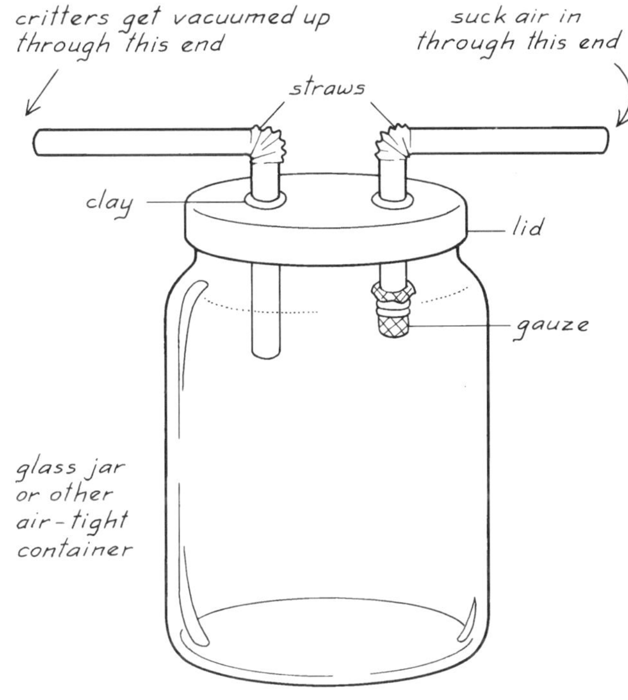

Arthropod vacuum

STEPS

Insect Vacuum

1. Make two straw-sized holes in the top of your container.
2. Insert the straws and use modeling clay, waterproof glue, or hot glue to hold them and fill any gaps.
3. Cover the inside tip of one straw with gauze and use a small rubber band to hold it.
4. Replace the lid and use the pooter to vacuum up and observe small insects. Just remember to suck on the covered straw. To help you remember, cut it shorter than the intake straw, or use different-colored straws.
5. Observe your critters in the jar or transfer them to your bugarium (see previous activity) for long-term observation.

Pitfall Trap

1. Bury the containers so their lips are at ground level.
2. Place different foods into each container. Put bits of fruit or meat in one and lettuce, tomato bits, or cheese into the other. Does fresh bait work better than older stuff?
3. Cover the traps to protect them from rain and large animals; use small stones to raise the cover off the ground slightly and allow insects to easily crawl in. If you use cardboard, put a rock or two on top to keep it from blowing away.
4. Leave the traps overnight, when no rain is expected, and check them at least once a day.
5. Experiment by putting out traps in various locations. Do you catch more insects in or near the garden, beside the brush pile, in an overgrown area, or beside the compost pile?

OTHER COLLECTORS

Tape a piece of paper into a funnel shape, so the small end is about finger size and the wide end is slightly larger than the opening of a wide-mouthed jar. Insert bait into such a jar. Tape the top of the funnel to the jar so the small end is a couple inches above the bottom of the jar. Use different baits—honey water, beer, soft drink, meat, fruit, vegetables—to attract and catch flying insects.

Open an umbrella and hold it upside down, or spread a large cloth under a tree and shake the limbs above. Sometimes insects will fall into your improvised "beating tray," making collection easier.

Arthropod vacuum in use

To make a joint-legged-critter net, follow the directions for making a dipping net (see Aquatic Critter Collector activity, page 97) and use nylon net (available from a sewing shop) instead of stockings. When you catch an insect, twist the net to close it and prevent escape.

FIND OUT MORE

See Monica Russo, *The Insect Almanac: A Year-Round Activity Guide* (New York: Sterling Publishing Co., 1991); Christopher Leahy, *Peterson First Guides: Insects* (Boston: Houghton Mifflin Co., 1987); and Gary Dunn, *Caring for Insect Livestock: An Insect Rearing Manual* and *Beginner's Guide to Observing and Collecting Insects*, both published by the Young Entomologists' Society (see the Butterfly Gardening entry, page 123, in the **Resources** listings).

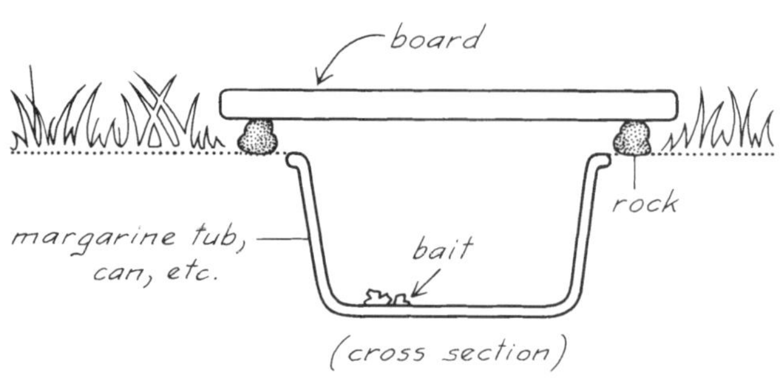

Pitfall trap

Tips and Tidbits

Arthropod is a Greek word meaning "jointed legs." This group includes not only insects but also arachnids, such as spiders and scorpions; horseshoe crabs; centipedes; millipedes; and crustaceans, such as lobsters and roly-polies. Arthropods have segmented bodies and paired legs with many joints. Insects have six legs, three distinct body segments, and two antennae; arachnids have eight legs, usually two body segments, and no antennae.

If you want to look at a captive insect and it won't hold still, put it in the refrigerator for a few minutes. Cool temperatures make arthropods slow down.

Some people use the word "bugs" for both insects and other arthropods. True bugs are a distinct group of insects—including giant waterbugs, water scorpions, stinkbugs, and bedbugs—that eat by piercing and sucking plant or animal fluids.

FEED A PRAYING MANTIS

LEVEL: Pathfinder (low; about ½ hour)

SEASONS: Summer and fall

MATERIALS:
Praying mantis (in the wild or caged)
Tweezers, forceps, needle-nose pliers, or toothpicks
Live insects (crickets, Japanese beetles, etc.)

INTRODUCTION

Praying mantises rank high among a gardener's insect friends. They are voracious predators of other insects, many of which are pests. Their strategy: Sit and wait. You can shorten their wait by offering them crickets or other small insects, which they often will devour before your eyes. You'll see that praying mantises don't waste anything—they even eat the back legs. They do, though, pass on the wings of grasshoppers and some other insects.

STEPS

1. Find a praying mantis in your yard. These insects roam shrubs and other garden plants. Look carefully, because they can be brown or green and may look just like a leaf or stem.

   When threatened, a praying mantis may hop away or rear up on its hind legs and try to look bigger and more ferocious. Sometimes they fly for short distances.
2. To feed these garden helpers, have one backyard entomologist guard the mantis so it doesn't get away, while the other collects some insects of various sizes.
3. Using tweezers or other long pincers, offer the mantis a meal. It may take a while, but if the bait is alive, the mantis will probably take it eventually.
4. Watch how the predator eats its prey—almost like an ear of corn.
5. Experiment with different insect foods.

   If you don't have any holding tools, use a toothpick or use your fingers. Hand-feeding may not work, though; after all, a human hand looks mighty big to a praying mantis. You have to be very still, and be careful, because the prey-grasping spines on the mantis's forelegs can be painful.

The praying mantis is a lightning-fast hunter.

Mantis Egg Cases

Add beneficial praying mantises to your backyard. In the fall and spring, comb wildflower patches and fields for light-brown praying mantis egg cases. Bring them back to your yard, and tie them securely to a shrub. See the **Resources** listing, page 126, for other ways to get praying mantis egg cases.

Newly emerged praying mantises rest before spreading out to avoid being eaten.

FIND OUT MORE

See Bianca Lavies, *Backyard Hunter: Praying Mantis* (New York: Dutton, 1990) (for young readers); and Ken Preston-Mafham, *Grasshoppers and Mantids of the World,* (New York: Facts On File, 1990) (for older readers).

Tips and Tidbits

The female praying mantis usually eats her partner after mating. Sometimes she starts snacking while they are mating, and she may eat several would-be mates before finally mating. She will lay her egg case on a twig about 21 days later in a brown foam that hardens into a protective papery case about the size of a Brazil nut.

In spring, praying mantises emerge from eggs laid in the fall. As they grow, they may compete with each other for food and even eat their own brothers and sisters. If you find several on one bush, catch all but one or two and distribute them around your backyard.

If you want to keep a praying mantis for observation, feed it a live insect at least four times a day and spray some water on the plants in the cage every day. In captivity, praying mantises can live nine months. In the wild, they may live six months.

In addition to insects, praying mantises will eat wet dog or cat food, or gourd meat. Large mantises have been known to eat small frogs, salamanders, lizards, and even hummingbirds.

Praying mantises are cousins of walkingsticks, grasshoppers, crickets, cockroaches, and katydids.

BUILD A HABITAT FOR THE HARMLESS

LEVEL: Naturalist/Explorer (medium/high; about 3 hours)

SEASONS: All

MATERIALS:
(22) 1" roundhead wood screws
(2) 1" #6 flathead wood screws
(2) 2" #6 flathead wood screws
1" × 2″ (actual size ¾" × 1½") × 53" wood
2 panes of Plexiglas, each 12" × 16"
Scrap wood for a base, approximately ¾" × 6" × 18"
Brace and bit or drill and 7/64" bit (it helps to have a #6 countersinking drill bit, so the frame's corner and base screws go in flush, without cracking the wood)
Screwdriver
Medium sandpaper and sanding block or wood rasp
Waterproof glue

OPTIONAL
Clamp
Right-angle clamps or square
Waterproof aquarium glue
White candle (unscented), varnish, polyurethane, or boiled linseed oil

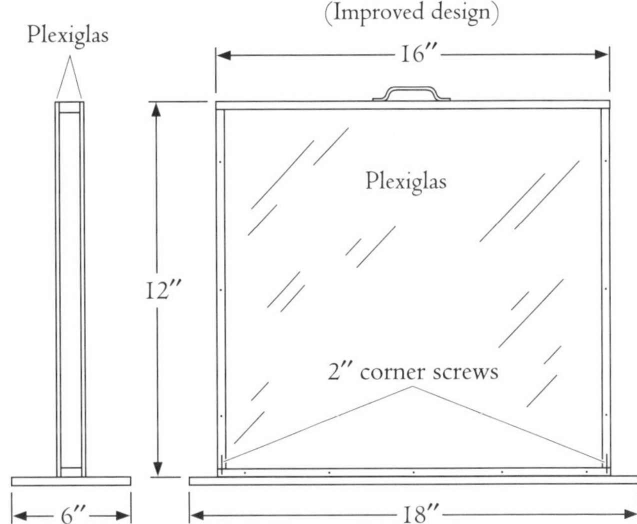

Plan for Habitat for the Harmless observatory

INTRODUCTION

On those days when the weather is uncooperative, it's nice to be able to observe wild creatures from the comfort of your warm, dry room. Not only that, many activities of the insect world take place underground, which makes observation difficult for humans. Build an observatory that can be used many different ways—as an ant or beetle farm, Worm-a-rama (see activity, page 15), worm-composting experimentation station, bugatorium, or miniature terrarium/rootatorium (for observing the roots of plants).

STEPS

1. Cut the 1 × 2-inch wood into sections: two 10½-inch segments (sides), and two 16-inch segments (bottom and top).
2. Glue the frame together (see diagram), leaving out the 16-inch cover. Use right-angle clamps or a square to maintain the right angles.
3. Drill pilot holes and drive a screw at both bottom corners (see diagram).
4. Sand sharp or rough corners with medium sandpaper.
5. Rub the inside of the frame with wax, or coat it with polyurethane, varnish, or boiled linseed oil to protect the wood.
6. When glue has set, place Plexiglas over one side, drill 11 pilot holes (clamp the Plexiglas in place if necessary), and drive the roundhead screws.
7. Turn the observatory over, making sure the

Plexiglas on the underside is protected from scratches. Repeat previous step. To prevent leakage, you can use aquarium glue to seal the Plexiglas to the frame.

8. If Plexiglas edges and corners are rough or sharp, use a sanding block to smooth them without scratching the Plexiglas.
9. Glue or screw the 18-inch base to the observatory.
10. Attach a knob or a scrap of wood on the top for a handle.

Ants from two colonies fight it out. For an ant farm, you must have the queen.

FIND OUT MORE

See Judy Braus, ed., *Ranger Rick's NatureScope: Incredible Insects* (Vienna, VA: National Wildlife Federation, 1989). See also the **Resources** listing, page 126.

Tips and Tidbits

Keep tabs on your harmless inhabitants. Use a notebook to record what they do and when you started observing them.

Experiment with your harmless inhabitants by offering them different foods and watching their reactions. To prevent mold, remove any food that isn't eaten.

Most underground dwellers prefer darkness, so cover your container with a dark cloth when you're not observing its residents.

ATTRACT MOTHS AT NIGHT

LEVEL: Pathfinder (low; about 1 hour)

SEASONS: Late spring, summer, and early fall

MATERIALS:

Portable light fixture (such as a work light)
Outdoor extension cord
White bedsheet
String
Clothespins
Bricks or other weights to anchor sheet on the ground
Container for collecting moths (see Bugarium activity, page 51)
Baits (brown sugar and water, molasses, fruit juice, maple syrup)
Several bait holders (bottle caps, jar lids, etc.)

OPTIONAL
Cloth strips
Banana or peaches and water
Flashlight

INTRODUCTION

Night-loving moths are much more numerous than daylight-loving butterflies. There are about 10 times as many moths as butterflies in the world. Not all moths are nocturnal, but most are. Many of them also use light to navigate in the dark. That means the best time to collect moths is at night, and the best way to do it is to use a light.

STEPS

1. This activity works best when there is little wind or chance of rain. If you have an outdoor light that's not out of reach, use that. If not, use an outdoor extension cord and a work light or other portable fixture.
2. Hang a white bedsheet within a few feet of the light and anchor the ends. If you are using a floodlight, point it toward the sheet. Make sure to hang the sheet so that a couple feet extend in front on the ground. This makes for easier collection when insects hit the sheet and fall to the ground.
3. Check the cloth several times during the night and collect some moths for observation.
4. Remember to bring the experiment inside before you go to bed.
5. Moths can be attracted not only by light but by scents. Try adding some tubs (bottle caps will do) filled with sweets of different kinds: brown sugar and water, molasses, honey, fruit juice, and maple syrup. Put out one cap with everything mixed together. Also set out a mashed banana or peach bits mixed with water. You may have better luck if you soak strips of cloth in the various mixtures and hang them near the sheet.
6. See which bait attracts the most moths. Spread the best bait on a dead tree or fence post for a few nights running.
7. Check the bait every hour and record any activity.
8. In the morning, look around the light/bait station again for stragglers. Look in shaded, protected areas.
9. To prove that the moths aren't attracted only to the light, repeat the experiment sometime, with no light (except a flashlight, so you can check the baits).

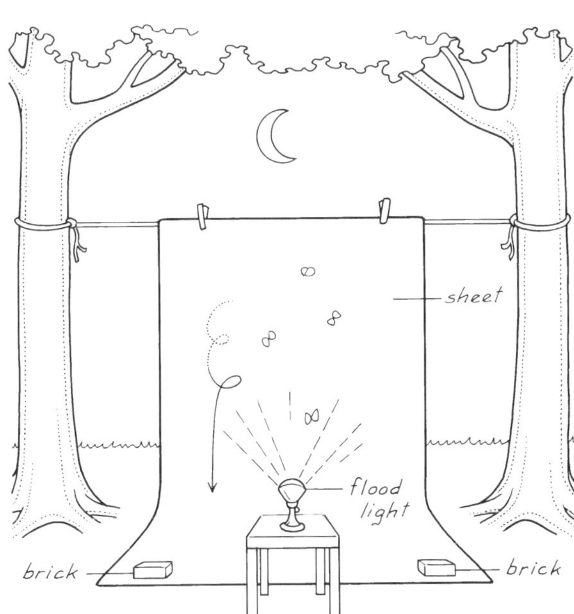

Attract moths on a windless night using a sheet and a floodlight.

A large maple spanworm caterpillar (only about an inch long) looks just like a stem. Its head is below.

TAKE THE NEXT STEP

Collect some moths in a screened cage. Remove all baits and lights and set the cage out overnight. Check every hour. Are other moths attracted? If so, you must have at least one female in the cage. Male moths are attracted to subtle female scents called pheromones. That's why some male moths have larger antennae that their female counterparts. They need them to smell the female's perfume, which they can detect from more than a mile away. Pheromones are also used by some other insects; ants use them to mark important trails.

Find Out More

See Lynn M. Stone, *Moths* (Vero Beach, FL: Rourke Corp., 1993); and Charles V. Covell Jr., *A Field Guide to the Moths of Eastern North America* (Peterson Field Guide Series; Boston: Houghton Mifflin Co., 1984).

Tips and Tidbits

Many moths are important pollinators of night-flowering plants.

When handling moths or butterflies, cup your hands around them to avoid damaging the wings.

Some moths look like other creatures. The Doll's clearwing moth looks like a wasp. This brand of mimicry protects it from some predators. The hummingbird moth is often mistaken for its namesake. Its fan-shaped tail makes it look like it has tail feathers.

Usually, any moths you catch will have already mated. Feed them sugar water and/or mashed fruit mixed with water and see if they lay eggs.

Inchworms are not worms, but caterpillars, which turn into a kind of moth, part of the geometer family.

The cecropia is the largest North American moth, with a wingspan of nearly 6 inches. The Hercules moth of Australia has a wingspan of about 10 inches, making it one of the world's largest insects. Both belong to the giant silk moth family. Adults of these species do not eat at all, but only mate and die.

Mammals

Build a House for Bats

LEVEL: Naturalist/Explorer (medium/high; 2 hours)

SEASONS: All; mount before spring

MATERIALS:

WOOD

½" × 2" × 4" (exterior plywood is recommended, but any rough-surfaced wood will do; never use treated lumber for wildlife)

1" × 2" (actual size ¾" × 1¾") × 8' furring strip

HARDWARE

Saw (hand or circular)

Square

⅛" plastic (*not* metal) netting 20" × 22½"

Scissors

Staple gun with 5⁄16" galvanized, exterior staples (or tacks)

Screwdriver

(20) 1⅝" drywall screws and (10) 1⅛" screws (you can use a hammer and 4d galvanized steel finishing nails, but they won't hold as well)

Drill and 3⁄16" bit for drilling pilot holes, #6 countersink bit (for screws)

Acrylic caulking

1 pint acrylic latex paint: black or dark brown in moderate to cool climates (to absorb warmth), tan to white in hot regions

Paintbrush

Clamps

INTRODUCTION

Many people are afraid of bats, but the world's only winged mammals pose little threat to humans. They rarely transmit rabies to humans and never get caught in people's hair. Bats are not only misunderstood, they are suffering from rapid habitat loss.

We should welcome backyard bats because they do us the great service of gobbling up pesky insects. A single bat may eat 600 mosquitos an hour and upwards of 7,000 insects a night. In fact, bats are among the most proficient nocturnal predators of mosquitos and other night-flying insects.

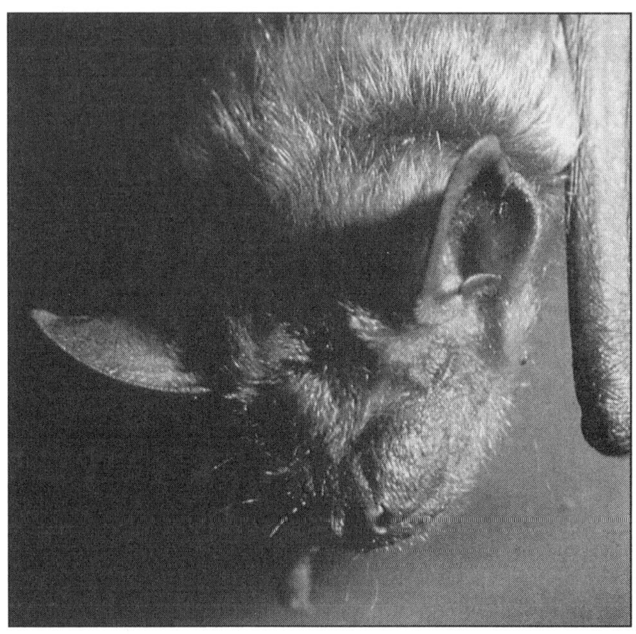

The little brown bat is a common bat house resident in most of North America.

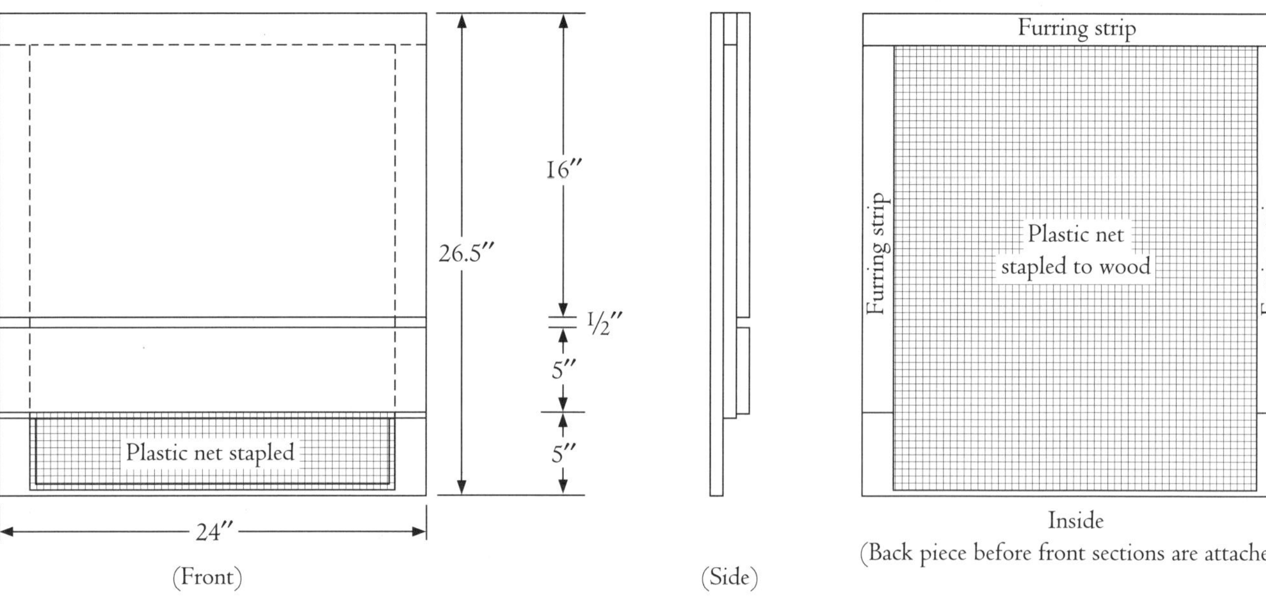

Diagram of a bat house. Scratches inside provide footing for bats, making the netting unnecessary.

Help your local bats feel at home by building them a house. In return, they will help control biting insects.

STEPS

(The following plan is adapted from the *The Bat House Builder's Handbook;* see **Find Out More.**)

1. Cut three pieces of 24-inch-wide plywood to the following lengths: 26½ inches (back), 16½ inches (front top), and 5 inches (front bottom). If your plywood is slightly less than 48 inches long, the front-bottom piece can be shorter.
2. Cut the 1 × 2-inch wood into three pieces, one 24 inches long and two 20¼ inches long.
3. Squeeze caulk on one wide surface of the 24-inch-long furring strip and attach it with screws or nails along the top of the back piece, then caulk and attach the side pieces. The caulk prevents drafts, which bats can't tolerate.
4. Staple netting to the inside surface of the back, starting at the bottom. This provides a surface that the bats can cling to. Make sure netting lies flat without puckering, or it might stretch and block access to the house. You can also use a saw or chisel to make horizontal grooves about an inch apart on the inside surfaces of the back wall. This will make the netting unnecessary.
5. Caulk the facing wide surfaces of the furring strips and attach the front-top section.
6. Attach the front-bottom section, leaving a ½-inch space between it and the top-front piece. This should leave about a 4½ -inch landing lip at the back. Allow caulk to dry and cure.
7. Paint with two or three coats (see color suggestions below).
8. To mount the house, you may want to attach a piece of scrap wood to the back. This should be less than an inch thick, 2 to 4 inches wide, and about 30 inches long.

Mount the house on a pole or on the side of a building, 12 to 20 feet above ground (bats seem to prefer the higher elevations). Orientation (which direction the house faces) depends on your climate: Houses in moderate to cool climates should face south for maximum exposure to the sun; in very hot regions, houses should not receive more than about six hours of sun a day.

Long Term

If bats don't take to your house after two seasons, make minor adjustments in color (darker or lighter) or orientation (more or less sun). If no bats move in after several minor changes, try a new location.

Find Out More

See Merlin D. Tuttle and Donna L. Hensley, *The Bat House Builder's Handbook* (Austin, TX: Bat Conservation International, 1993). Also from BCI: an educator's activity book, a video, and *America's Neighborhood Bats,* by Merlin D. Tuttle (Austin, TX: University of Texas Press, 1988). To order merchandise or receive information about participating in the North American Bat House Research Project, see the **Resources** listing, page 126.

Example of a larger (and much heavier) bat house

Tips and Tidbits

At least nine North American bat species use bat houses. Of these, big and little brown bats are the most common occupants throughout most of the United States and Canada. In the South, Mexican free-tailed bats predominate.

Bat houses within 1,000 feet of a stream, marsh, or pond have the best chance of being occupied.

You don't have to clean your bat house, but you should remove any wasp nests in the winter.

Daytime temperatures inside a bat house need to be between 85° and 100°F.

Bats do not compete in any way with birds.

The only blood-loving bats are the vampire bats of Latin America, which prey on large mammals and birds and actually lap, rather than suck, the blood of their victims.

Bat dung, called guano, is jam-packed with nitrogen and other minerals, making it an excellent fertilizer. It also was processed to make gunpowder during the Civil War. Collect it and put it on your compost pile.

One colony of 20 million Mexican free-tailed bats in Texas consumes an estimated 250 tons of insects a night.

Make a Squirrel Feeder and a Nest Box

LEVEL: Naturalist/Explorer (medium/high; about 1 hour)

SEASONS: All

MATERIALS:

FOR CHAIN FEEDER
Rope or chain, 2' to 3' long
Eye screw (about 3")
Dried corn on the cob

FOR MULTIPLE FEEDER
1" × 2" × 4' furring strip
Several long screws or nails

FOR NEST BOX
1" × 10" × 8' board
Drill and 3" drill bit (or use a saw for square hole) and ¼" bit
6d finishing nails or 1½" #6 flathead screws (use a #6 countersinking bit for screws)

INTRODUCTION

Some people object to squirrels at bird feeders, especially when they hog the birdseed. In fact, an entire industry is devoted to making and selling squirrel-excluding devices for bird feeders. But the chattersome and acrobatic rodents can be entertaining to watch, and they are often the most abundant wild mammals in the neighborhood. Certainly they are among the most conspicuous backyard mammals active during the daytime. Besides, offering squirrels a feeding station of their own may divert them from your bird feeders.

A gray squirrel at a board-mounted feeder.

STEPS

Platform Feeder

Any simple tree-mounted platform feeder will suit squirrels. They are not picky. This can be similar to the nesting platform (see page 35) or the feeding platform (see page 40). But a variety of other feeders can be made from scrap wood.

Chain Feeder

One of the simplest squirrel feeders is a 2- or 3-foot length of rope or chain with a 3-inch or so eye screw attached to the end. Screw it into a dried ear of corn and hang it from a tree limb.

Multiple, Board-Mounted Feeder

A multiple feeder can be made from a 4-foot piece of 1 × 2-inch wood.

1. Drive four or five long nails or screws (at least 3 inches long) into the wood, so that the sharp ends protrude.
2. Paint or stain the wood, if desired.
3. Put ears of dried corn on each point and mount the feeder at about shoulder height between two posts or trees, with the cobs pointing up.

Box Feeder

You can also make a tree-mounted box with a hinged top to hold peanuts, corn kernels, or other squirrel food. Include a sitting platform jutting out at the bottom. When you mount it, put a piece of food between the lid and the box to attract the squirrels.

Nest Box

(Adapted from *Woodworking for Wildlife;* see **Find Out More** on page 38.) The squirrel nest box is similar to the birdhouse on page 37, but even easier to make.

1. From an 8-foot-long, 1 × 10-inch board, cut a 22-inch back, 16-inch front and sides, a 12-inch top, and a 7¾-inch bottom. (If your wood is ⅞ inch thick (as cedar often is), the bottom should be 7½ inches long.)
2. Cut the 3-inch entrance hole on the side, so its edges are about 2 inches from the top and an inch from the back. Alternatively, cut a 3 × 3-inch square entrance hole in the upper rear corner.
3. Drill two ¼-inch holes for ventilation in the opposite side and four for drainage in the bottom.
4. Put the box together with nails or screws.

   Don't worry about making a swing door—unlike most birds, squirrels will build over an old nest or redo it to their own satisfaction, so their boxes don't need to be cleaned. Before sealing it up, though, you may want to fill it halfway with leaves to provide a welcome mat.
5. Mount it directly to a tree using screws (don't use wire, which eventually would harm the tree), at least 15 feet above ground. If possible, mount it so it rests on a limb, with the back attached to the tree trunk. The nest box should be mounted in fall for winter use.

Find Out More

See Jana McConoughey, *The Squirrels* (Mankato, MN: Crestwood House, 1983).

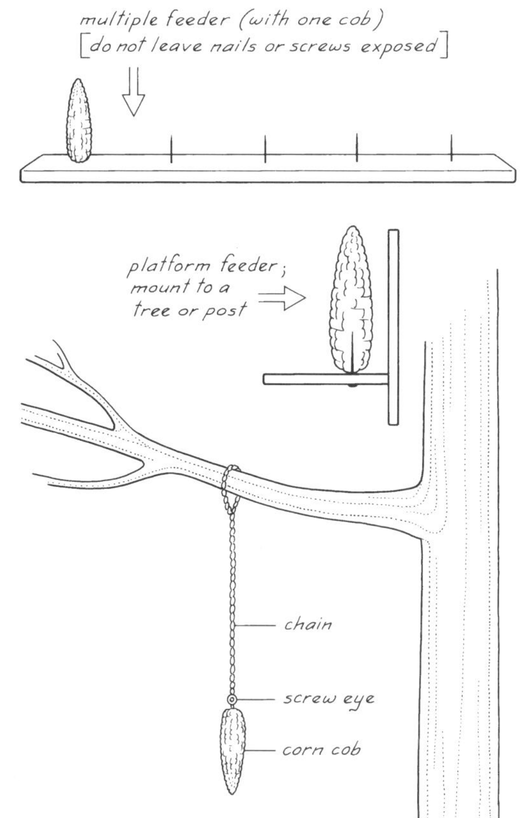

Two of many kinds of squirrel feeders: chain- and board-mounted versions.

Tips and Tidbits

Gray squirrels do not hibernate, but remain active in winter, which is when they mate. Two or three babies are born about 40 days later. Many squirrels mate again in summer.

This 4-week-old gray squirrel was abandoned by its mother when their nest-tree was cut down. It was hand-raised and later returned to the wild.

At birth, squirrels are hairless, blind, deaf, and weigh about half an ounce—less than two nickels. In about a month, their eyes and ears will have opened, and they will be covered with hair.

In addition to seeds, berries, buds, and nuts, squirrels also eat insects and tree sap, as well as the occasional planted bulb. Squirrels sometimes eat mushrooms. In fact, they can eat some kinds of mushrooms that are poisonous to humans. Squirrels eat an average of 2 pounds of food a week, more than 100 pounds a year.

Although gray squirrels will sometimes rob bird nests, they are not as aggressive as red squirrels. Luckily for backyard songbirds, red squirrels prefer deep woodlands to open gardens.

Most squirrels are territorial, so one or two nest boxes per acre is probably all that will be used.

Flying squirrels don't really fly, but glide on flaps of skin. They inhabit the eastern half of the United States and most of Canada.

Build a Snow Shelter

LEVEL: Explorer (high; several hours)

SEASONS: Winter

MATERIALS:
Snow shovel
Spade
Scoops and digging tools: trowels, three-pronged gardening tool
Snow-removal containers: buckets, 18-gallon plastic storage containers, etc.
Warm gloves (may need several pairs)
Insulators: thick cardboard, foam rubber, newspapers wrapped in trash bags, blanket, etc.
Candles

OPTIONAL
Snowblower

INTRODUCTION

Just about every energetic youngster blessed with a heavy snowfall has attempted to make an igloo. This is a cinch for people of the Far North, but not for first-timers, unless the snow can be packed and cut into blocks. The usual result of such efforts is ice-cold hands and a fort.

With a little adult help (actually, a lot of help), the goal of building a snow shelter can be accomplished. This is not a true igloo, but it can be made with just about any kind of snow, and you don't have to be an Inuit or an architect to make it.

Building a snow shelter not only illustrates snow's excellent insulating properties, it provides an object of neighborhood pride and fond memories for the whole family.

STEPS

1. Create a monster mound of snow, 10 to 15 feet in diameter and about 7 feet tall. A snowblower makes this task much easier. You can make the pile smaller, but the roomy model described here can accommodate several adults and children.
2. Add an entrance pile about 4 feet high and 3 or 4 feet long. Part of the piling-up job can be accomplished when you shovel the sidewalk—just toss the snow all in one place, or rig a sled so your fellow workers can more easily transport the crystalline building material to the construction site.
3. You don't need to pack the snow. Just leave it overnight, and cold temperature and the pressure of the snow's weight will cause the snow to bind together into a hard dome.
4. Starting at the entrance, hollow out the structure with whatever tools work best for you. Use foam rubber pads, a small stack of newspapers

wrapped in a trash bag, or a blanket to protect your knees and other body parts from the moisture and cold. When you see light through the snow, you've reached the correct thickness, which is about 4 inches.

5. Remove the loose snow by piling it on a snow shovel or a thin sheet of cardboard and hauling it out through the entrance. Have your kids dump this around the sides of the shelter or use it to make a fort or another monster pile. Eventually, you'll be able to use larger digging tools and fit a container inside for snow removal, both of which speed up the process.

   The hollowing-out and snow removal work can be even more exhausting than the piling up part. Pace yourself, and take regular breaks to replenish fluids and change into dry clothes. When you can stand and swing a snow shovel inside, the pace really begins to accelerate.
6. Only after the roof is finished and the danger of collapse is past should you allow younger workers inside to help with the hollowing-out work. They can carve small benches and shelves into the sides.
7. Make a fist-sized hole in the roof for ventilation.
8. When the shelter is finished, use garden-furniture cushions or other insulation for seats (and feet). Insert thin wood slats into the shelter's sides and use them as candle-holding shelves or put several candles in the center. This gives the shelter the feel of an altar and makes it glow warmly at night. Obviously, you must be very careful around the candles. Invite family and friends to share hot chocolate, dessert, and the solemn quiet of a snow shelter.

Take the Next Step

Take temperature readings inside and outside the snow shelter. Note the inside temperature again after several people have been in the shelter for a while. How much does the shelter warm up after candles have been burning for an hour?

A good-sized snow shelter can accommodate several adults and children.

Tips and Tidbits

Unless you live in high elevations or northern regions, where daytime temperatures rarely exceed 32°F in wintertime, choose your site well. Opt for the north side of your house, where the shelter will be shaded from the sun. It's sad to spend so much time on a shelter, only to have it shrink and melt within a couple of days.

For safety, only adults should perform the initial hollowing-out work, and someone should always be on the outside, in case the dome collapses. Such a collapse is not likely to pose a serious risk for a healthy adult, but the weight of that much snow could trap a child. Once the inside is hollowed out, very little snow remains, and the danger is negligible.

Depending on the weather and how much sun your shelter receives, expect it to gradually shrink. In mildly cold weather and full sun, it may shrink nearly a foot a day before it collapses and melts.

Snow insulates so well because the crystals are surrounded by pockets of air, an excellent insulator.

The snowy winter habitat of field mice and other small mammals is called the subnivean (under-the-snow) layer.

Set Up a Brush Pile

LEVEL: Pathfinder (low; ½ hour)

SEASONS: All, but especially important in fall or winter

MATERIALS:

Several large rocks, fireplace logs, or cinder blocks
Brush, old Christmas trees, leaves
Soil

INTRODUCTION

Mammals need cover and shelter for safety from predators and as a place to raise young. Create a year-round home for several kinds of mammals and other wildlife simply by maintaining a brush pile in your backyard habitat. (This is a great, low-maintenance Kids' Corner project.)

Making a brush pile may sound self-explanatory, but there are several important considerations. For instance, it should not be too close to bird feeders, because it could provide cover for predatory cats. It should not be put directly next to the house, where it could cause a fire hazard. You also want to find a location where it will not be an eyesore to your neighbors.

In addition, you can make the brush pile more attractive to larger wildlife, such as rabbits, simply by creating a proper foundation with living spaces. The more you know about wildlife needs, the better you can help create an inviting habitat.

Once your brush pile is inhabited, you can watch the residents come and go or maybe even explore it once a year to find out what animals are using your habitat hotel.

STEPS

1. Lay down a floor of rocks to form a central living area and a maze of tunnels at least 6 inches high. This will provide living spaces and multiple entrances and exits. Now you need some covering—a "roof" to maintain these crawl spaces.
2. Cover the floor with scrap tin or use natural materials, such as straight, sturdy branches, laid as close together as possible.
3. Top that with a second and third layer of branches (each laid crosswise).
4. Cover this with a thick layer of leaves or dense brush, such as evergreen branches.
5. Atop that, pile dirt, vines, and branches to form an attractive beaver-den-like pile.

By creating protected spaces at the bottom of the pile, you also create a well-insulated home that offers protection from rain. Even if no rabbits move in, birds will probably use the brush pile as a shelter on windy, snowy days or as a nesting site and nighttime roost.

Other brush-pile foundation ideas: Use a stump as a centerpiece, laying strong branches on top like bicycle spokes. Lay several cinder blocks or sections of drain pipe to create a ground floor. Use a Christmas tree or a fallen tree (still attached to its stump, if possible) to create a tentlike brush pile.

Brush-pile Marketing

Sometimes, when faced with disapproving neighbors, it helps to use a little marketing. "Brush pile" may sound too sloppy or haphazard for some. Have your kids christen it with an amusing name, such as Lizard's Lodge, The Hop-Inn, Cottontail Club & Condo, Rabbit Roundhouse, or other more palatable terms. They can paint a sign and put it up in front of the brush pile to make it official.

Tips and Tidbits

Grow a live brush pile: Plant a half-dozen rose or forsythia shrubs in a tight group, care for them the first year so they get a healthy start, then let them grow wild. Bonica rose and serviceberry (amelanchier), which belongs to the rose family, are good for this purpose. You can also provide live cover around your homemade brush pile. Transplant honeysuckle vines, raspberries, and blackberries around a brush pile to help hide it and create a living, growing, edible brush pile.

In addition to rabbits and birds, your brush pile might make a home for chipmunks, toads, and voles.

PRESERVE TRACKS IN PLASTER

LEVEL: Naturalist (medium; about 1 hour)

SEASONS: All

MATERIALS:

Plaster of Paris
Container for mixing plaster
Large can with both ends removed, or tape and a 2"-wide strip of cardboard or a 2"-wide cross section of a milk jug (paper or plastic)
Paper and pencil or pen
Old toothbrush

OPTIONAL

Ruler or measuring tape
Petroleum jelly
Oil-based paint

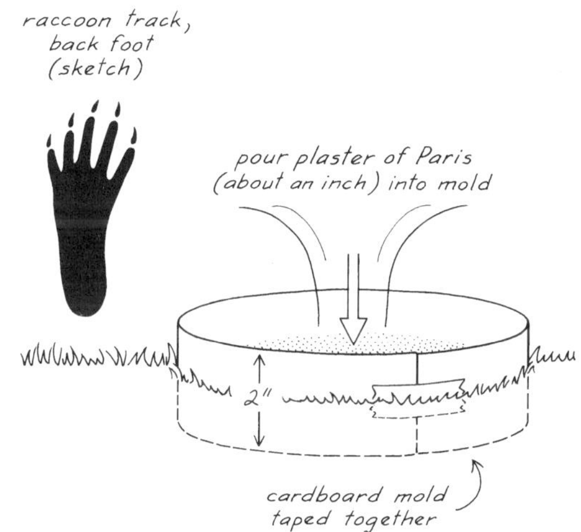

Raccoon track and example of a cardboard mold for preserving tracks in plaster.

INTRODUCTION

Traces of mammals surround us, but we don't always notice them. Such traces as scent are usually too faint for our noses to detect. Others, such as a tuft of hair caught in a fence, may or may not be seen. Mammals and many other animals also leave tracks, but unless they are walking in mud or snow, they don't always leave a clear imprint.

Sometimes mammal tracks and other traces tell wildlife stories. More often, though, they offer only clues. By learning to read their hidden information and putting it together with other observations, you can make educated guesses about what animal made the tracks, why it made them, in what direction it was headed, and whether it was in a hurry.

Start learning about tracks by capturing one in plaster. If you live in an area with lots of mammals, you can build a collection of track casts for display on your wall.

STEPS

1. After a rain or a light snowfall, scour your backyard and neighborhood for mammal tracks. If you can't find anything else, look for dog or cat

prints, which resemble wild animal tracks. Of course, you can also make your own hand- and foot-tracks, or create imaginary tracks.

2. Choose the clearest imprint and remove any loose leaves, grass, or sticks.
3. Sketch the track, and make another drawing showing the pattern of tracks.
4. Measure and note the distances between the footprints, front-to-back and side-to-side.
5. Place a mold (can, cardboard strip, or milk jug cross section) around the track, and press it into the mud or snow, so no plaster can escape along the bottom.
6. Follow the directions on the container to mix the plaster to the consistency of honey and pour about a 1-inch layer into the mold.
7. Let the plaster set until it hardens, which takes at least 10 minutes.
8. Remove the cast from the mold and allow it to dry several hours.
9. Brush off dirt with an old toothbrush.
10. Your cast is inverted, meaning that the track sticks out from the surface. For a more realistic cast, repeat the above procedure to make a cast of your cast, but first smear the surface of your first cast with petroleum jelly.
11. If you plan to hang the finished product on the wall, put a wire loop in the top as you pour the second cast.
12. When the second cast is dry, separate the two casts and wipe the petroleum jelly off the final cast.
13. Use oil-based paint to color the track black and the background light brown, green, or white, and apply a clear lacquer protective coat.
14. Label the track, if you know who or what made it, and describe where and when you found it.
15. Hang the cast on the wall as is, or glue it to a small piece of wood for display.

Pouring plaster into the track cast

FIND OUT MORE

See Kathleen V. Kudlinski, *Animal Tracks and Traces* (New York: Franklin Watts, 1991) (for young readers); John Farrand Jr., *National Audubon Society Pocket Guide to Familiar Animal Tracks of North America* (New York: Alfred A. Knopf, 1995); Donald Stokes and Lillian Stokes, *Guide to Animal Tracking and Behavior* (Boston: Little, Brown and Co., 1986); and Paul Rezendes, *Tracking & the Art of Seeing: How to Read Animal Tracks & Sign* (Charlotte, VT: Camden House Publishing, 1992). The last two are for older readers.

Tips and Tidbits

Other mammal signs to look for include gnaw or nibble marks on nuts, tree branches, or trunks; burrows or shallow holes in the ground;

beaten pathways; broken snail shells; nests (some mammals make nests, too); and scat, or droppings.

With the exception of rabbits, chipmunks, and most tree squirrels, almost all backyard mammals are more active at night.

Different mammals tread on different parts of their feet. Humans, squirrels, and raccoons use the entire foot; cats and dogs walk on their toes; and deer walk on their hooves, which are modified toenails.

Look for tracks and other traces around water, in areas with abundant food sources, and around areas that are seldom used by humans. You may be able to attract raccoons or opossums by setting out dog or cat food at night. Make a track trap by putting the food in the middle of a muddy area.

Rabbit and squirrel tracks are easy to misread, because the back legs actually land in front of the forepaws. If you don't know how to read the tracks, you might follow them in the wrong direction.

Reptiles and Amphibians

CREATE AN OUTDOOR OBSERVATORY

LEVEL: Naturalist (medium; several hours)

SEASONS: Spring and summer

MATERIALS:

FOR POOL

Shovel
Half-barrel
Water plants
Frogs or other amphibians

FOR ROCK PILE OR WALL

Shovel
Large and small stones

INTRODUCTION

Many people still kill any snake on sight, even though most of them are harmless and prey on rodents and insects. In America, even the rare bite from a poisonous snake is not usually fatal to humans. Lizards and turtles also help keep insect populations in check. Unless you have a pond or stream on your property, amphibians are less frequent backyard visitors, but they share the reptiles' affinity for insects and other invertebrates. Of all amphibians, probably the toad is the most common backyard resident.

These creatures, collectively called herps, should be welcome guests in any backyard wildlife habitat. Creating a home for reptiles and amphibians will help attract other animals, as well, and the herp habitat can be combined with the brush pile or wild area described in earlier activities.

STEPS

Amphibian Pool

1. The best way to attract most amphibians is to build a pool (see the Baths entry, page 125, in the **Resources** listings). This could be part of a short, artificial stream with a recirculating pump, waterfalls, shallow pools for birds, and a deeper pool for amphibians, such as frogs or aquatic turtles. Alternatively, you could make a still-water pond by using PVC pool-liner or concrete, or by sinking a half-barrel, a naturally shaped Fiberglas pool, or other container in the ground. The pond should be in a shady spot that receives at least some sun during the day. It needn't be larger than about 3 × 4 feet. To protect the inhabitants during hibernation, the depth of the pool or pond should be at least 15 inches.
2. Add plants, to keep the water fresh, and insect-eating amphibians, to control mosquitos.

Clearly this project is a major undertaking, and there is no guarantee that amphibians will take up residence. Even if you release amphibians into the area, they might not stay.

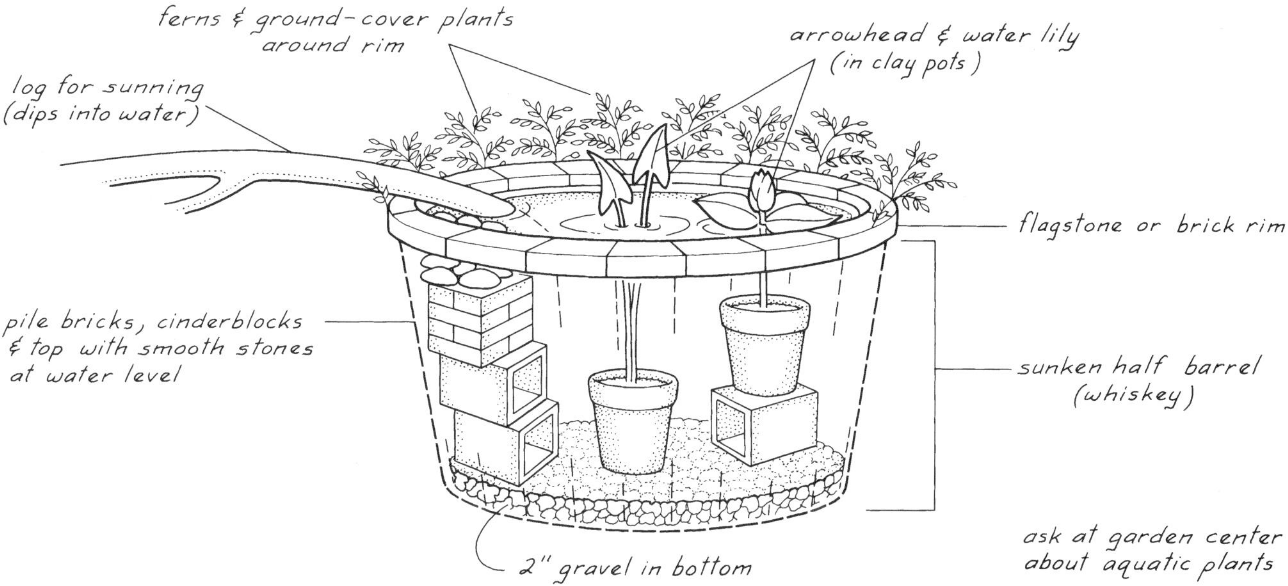

A sunken half-barrel can be made into habitat for amphibians and other animals.

Mini-Marsh

An alternative is to create a mini-marsh. In *The Backyard Naturalist,* Backyard Wildlife Habitat specialist Craig Tufts describes how he created a 450-square-foot marsh next to his suburban Washington, DC, home. In *Gardening for Wildlife* Tufts also gives details for making permanent water gardens.

Toad House

For a simple project, create a toad house. Toads are probably the easiest amphibians for which to provide outdoor housing. All they need is a cool, damp spot and a source of water. Find a shady area, dig a shallow hole, and partly cover it with a board or an overturned clay pot to provide a toad boarding house. Toads are among the few animals that eat destructive, plant-eating slugs as well as other garden pests.

Reptile/Amphibian Condo

Another snail-eater is the garter snake, and an excellent rodent- and insect-eater is the black rat snake. You may be able to lure not only toads and snakes but lizards and turtles as well by building a reptile and amphibian condominium. This can be a simple rock pile or low, unmortared stone wall. To make it cool, moist, and inviting, dig a shallow trench (no more than about 6 inches) where you plan to pile the rocks. As with the brush pile described in an earlier activity, you want to leave plenty of living space between and beneath the stones.

Find Out More

See Judy Braus, ed., *Ranger Rick's NatureScope: Let's Hear It for Herps* (Vienna, VA: National Wildlife Federation, 1987); and John L. Behler, *National Audubon Society Field Guide to North American Reptiles & Amphibians* (New York: Alfred A. Knopf, 1979).

Tips and Tidbits

People who study reptiles and amphibians are called herpetologists. The word comes from Greek roots meaning "creeping creature."

Toads do not have or spread warts—those bumps are glands.

Nearly 90 percent of a toad's diet consists of garden pests, and this nocturnal hunter may eat more than 10,000 per season.

Some of the more common lizards in North America are the slender glass and eastern fence lizards, racerunners (whiptails), and several species of skink.

Turtles, unlike snakes, supplement their diet of slugs, snails, and other pesky invertebrates with berries, tomatoes, lettuce, and other garden goodies.

During its 60- to 80-year lifetime, a box turtle rarely travels more than a mile from its birthplace.

Of about 115 snake species native to the United States and Canada, fewer than 20 are poisonous.

Other beneficial snakes that might visit your backyard are the insectivorous brown snake and rough or smooth green snake, and the carnivorous milk snake. All snakes are carnivorous, eating meat, eggs, and/or invertebrates exclusively. Many smaller snakes eat earthworms, as well as pest invertebrates. Some larger snakes, such as rat snakes, raid squirrel and bird nests.

SET UP AN INDOOR OBSERVATORY

LEVEL: Naturalist (medium; several hours)

SEASONS: Late spring, summer, and early fall

MATERIALS:

10-gallon or larger aquarium
Tight-fitting wire top
Foundation materials (depending on type of animal to be kept): large and small gravel, soil (garden soil, compost, leaf litter), peat, moss, and sand
Branches, twigs, or pieces of rotting wood
Pine needles, dry moss, or bark chips
Medium-sized stones
Shallow water container

OPTIONAL

Plants, such as ferns, small-leaved philodendron, slow-growing ivy, or other terrarium-suited plants (see terrarium activity, page 21)

INTRODUCTION

Having made your backyard habitat attractive to toads, garter snakes, and other beneficial reptiles and amphibians, you may discover them taking up residence. You may also want to observe them at closer quarters for a short time. Many reptiles and amphibians can be brought indoors for a few days of observation, but only if their basic needs are met. Taking hints from your captive's natural surroundings, you can create an inviting, temporary home for it.

STEPS

The habitat and dietary needs of various reptiles and amphibians vary quite a bit, so the more you learn about the animal you want to observe, the better you can anticipate its needs. The size of the container is the first consideration. For smaller specimens it should be at least a foot wide, 2 feet long, and a foot tall. A 10-gallon aquarium with a tight-fitting screen top is a good size. Of course, several smaller animals housed together or any larger animals need more room.

For Toads

1. Cover the container's bottom with about a half-inch of small gravel topped by another half-inch of larger gravel.
2. Add about 1 or 2 inches of damp soil mixed with peat, and cover it with a layer of moss.
3. Add rocks, pieces of rotting wood, and water.
4. Plants make an attractive addition to containers as well.

For Lizards and Snakes

1. Most of these reptiles require a drier environment. Spread about 2 inches of sand in the container and cover it with pine needles, dry moss, bark chips, or small gravel.
2. To add interest, make the surface uneven, with a few rocks and branches for the animals to slither and crawl around.
3. For easy access, bury the water source—a jar top or shallow bowl—to the rim in the sand. Use common sense with snakes: don't try to keep a 4-foot-long snake in a 2-foot-long container.

For Box Turtles

These reptiles require more room and are best kept in an outdoor turtle run. Better yet, let them roam freely in your backyard and put out some kitchen scraps for them, such as lettuce, tomato parts, overripe berries, and banana peels.

For tips on keeping salamanders and young newts, see the Streamside Creature Survey activity, page 91.

Most reptiles and amphibians need at least some sunlight. Put their container (vivarium) in indirect light, preferably in a north-facing window. Feed them regularly with a varied menu of worms, slugs, small bits of lean hamburger or other meat, and insects. Remove uneaten food before it spoils, and clean out the vivarium if it begins to smell.

Find Out More

See Tim Halliday and Kraig Adler, eds., *The Encyclopedia of Reptiles and Amphibians* (New York: Facts On File, 1986). For information on purchasing reptiles, amphibians, or vivaria for observation, see the **Resources** listing, page 126.

Tips and Tidbits

Change the water in your vivarium daily, using water that has been left out for a day (allowing copper ions and chlorine to dissipate). The water container should be large enough to accommodate bathing.

Remember, your goal in setting up a vivarium is to observe the inhabitants. Avoid excessive handling. Handling any wild animal is stressful for it and should be minimized.

Be selective if you want to put more than one reptile or amphibian in the same container. They may not be compatible, and one may kill the other.

Toads exude a mild toxin through their wartlike glands to help protect them from predators. This defense deters some predators, but not others, such as skunks and hognose snakes. The poison is not a danger to humans, but it can irritate the eyes, nose, and other mucous membranes. Always wash your hands after handling toads or any other wild animals.

Even some nonvenomous snakes will bite if handled, and an untreated wound can become infected. Use a snake hook or hold snakes with thumb and forefinger just behind the head. Turtles also may try to bite.

Some people buy gecko lizards and set them free in their house or apartment. The seldom-seen, nocturnal reptiles help control cockroaches and other unwelcome guests.

Trees

ADOPT A TREE

LEVEL: Pathfinder (low; about ½ hour each)

SEASONS: Summer and fall (some can also be done in winter and spring)

MATERIALS:
Backyard habitat map
Field guide to tree identification
Dark-colored crayon (peeled), and yellow, orange, red, or green crayons or markers
Paper
Yardstick
Tape measure
Graph paper

INTRODUCTION

Trees touch our lives in many ways. They provide a wealth of practical goods and aesthetic values, including lumber, oxygen, and sheer majesty. Around your house, they can reduce heating and cooling costs by helping to keep the house warmer in winter and cooler in summer. Tree roots anchor soil, reduce erosion, and help purify our water.

Trees also provide food and/or shelter for many other organisms, including birds, insects and other arthropods, worms, snails, squirrels, raccoons, fungi, lichens, and moss. During their various life stages, trees may host completely different communities of creatures.

Choose a backyard or neighborhood tree and learn as much as you can about it.

STEPS

1. Select a backyard or neighborhood tree, identify it, and mark it on your backyard habitat map.

Bark-rubbing tree model (dark, bark-side facing out)

Measuring a tree by yourself

2. Start a Treebook—a collection of photos and information about your tree—or incorporate one into your Backyard Habitat Album.
3. Make a model of your tree. **(a)** First, make a bark rubbing by placing a sheet of paper on the bark and rubbing it with the side of a dark crayon. If you have trouble holding the paper still, tie it to the trunk. **(b)** Color the other side green (or orange, yellow, and red, for fall). **(c)** Cut 3-inch-long and ¼-inch-wide strips along the top. **(d)** Roll the finished rubbing into a cylinder (with the rubbing on the outside) and make a model of your tree using tape, scissors, and cardboard.
4. Measure the height of your tree. This is not as hard as it may seem, but you need two people. **(a)** Have your child stand 20 yards (roughly 27 adult paces) from the tree, holding a yardstick with the end on the ground. **(b)** You lie down with your head 6 feet farther away from the yardstick, and—with your head as close to the ground as possible—note how the tree measures up. **(c)** Tell your child to move his or her free hand to where the yardstick and the treetop align. **(d)** Count the number of inches from the ground to the mark and multiply by 10, and you will have a good approximation of the tree's height in feet. **(e)** Switch places and try again to see if you get the same answer.

   You or your child can also take a measurement without any help. **(a)** Tie a band or ribbon around the trunk 5 feet from the ground. **(b)** Back up several yards and, holding a stick at arm's length, use your thumb to mark the distance on the stick from the ground to the band with your thumb. **(c)** Count how many of these measurements it takes to bridge the distance from ground to treetop, multiply by 5, and that's the approximate height in feet.
5. If your tree is mature—not just a sapling—you can estimate its age. You don't need to cut it down and count the rings (please don't!). Measure its trunk girth (circumference) about 5 feet from the ground. On average, a tree's girth increases an inch a year. Exceptions to this rule are fast-growing poplars and some pines, slow-growing chestnut trees, and any tree whose growth has been stunted by disease, shade from nearby trees, or other causes.

   It's easier to guess the age of pine trees. They

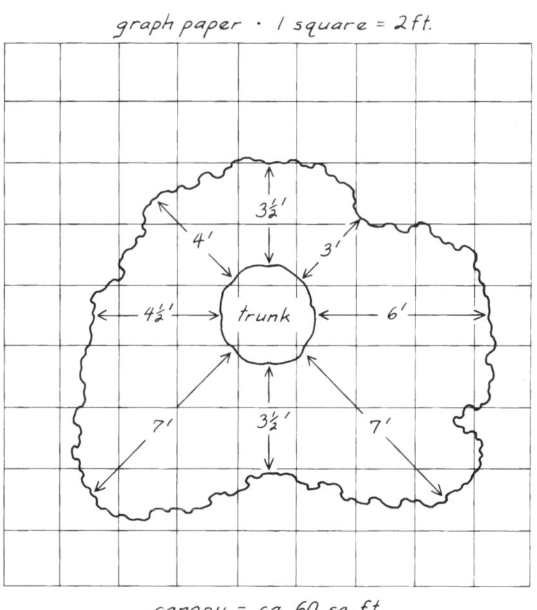

Measuring the canopy is a bit complicated.

put out a spoked set of branches (whorls) every year. Just count the number of branch whorls, and that's the age (unless someone has cut off a layer).

6. Measure your tree's canopy—the leafy part of a tree that is also known as the crown. **(a)** Wait till about one o'clock on a sunny summer day, when a strong shadow falls directly below the tree. **(b)** Use a tape measure or count paces along the outer edge of the canopy's shadow to find its circumference. **(c)** Finding the area is trickier. Measure the distance from the trunk to the canopy's edge in at least eight directions. **(d)** Make a scale map on graph paper, so that each box represents I foot. You'll have to approximate the shape of the canopy. **(e)** Now count the boxes to get the canopy's square footage.

FIND OUT MORE

See Tony Secunda and John Goodchild, *Grow Your Own Trees: A Book & Seeds* (New York: Marlowe & Co., 1995).

Tips and Tidbits

Make it official. Create an adoption certificate with a description of your chosen tree, its vital statistics (including identification), and date of adoption. Paint a wooden identification plaque for your tree and hang it with a chain around the trunk.

Try to visit your adopted tree once a month for a year. Take photographs of it from the same position in each of the four seasons. Date the pictures and include them in your Treebook.

Bark patterns can help you identify a tree.

LEAF PRINTING

LEVEL: Pathfinder (low; about ½ hour each)

SEASONS: All

MATERIALS:

FOR RUBBINGS AND STENCILS
Leaves (the flatter, the better)
Paper
Markers, crayons, pencils, or paints

OPTIONAL
Old toothbrush

FOR RUBBINGS
Acrylic paints
Paintbrush
Art roller (brayer), rolling pin, or large spoon
Paper
Newspaper or paper towel

FOR COLLAGES
White glue

INTRODUCTION

Leaves are a tree's energy gatherers, food factories, lungs, and "sweat glands." Although trees don't actually sweat, they do give off moisture. Leaves are wonderful studies in delicacy and strength. After they leave the tree, they decay, providing nutrients that are absorbed by the tree roots eventually—recycling at its best.

Through the ages, people have used leaves as bedding, insulation, decorations, and symbols. Greeks and Romans in ancient times awarded a crown of laurel (also known as sweet bay) as a symbol of achievement, hence the expression "to rest on one's laurels." This also is the origin of "baccalaureate," meaning the berry of the laurel.

Leaves also offer us many possibilities for art and craft projects. The following is just a small sampling. With a little thought, you can come up with many more.

STEPS

1. Make leaf rubbings. **(a)** Place one or more leaves (veins up) on a smooth surface (newspaper sections work well). **(b)** Cover them with a sheet of paper. **(c)** Rub over them with a crayon, marker, or the side of a pencil.
2. Make leaf stencils by arranging the leaves on a sheet of paper and using a soft marker or paintbrush to color the outlines. A fun but messy technique is to dip an old toothbrush into paint, and use your thumb or a stick to splatter dots of color on and around the leaves. When you finish the stencil, use a different color to decorate the white part that was covered by the leaf, or put the leaf beneath the paper and make a rubbing.
3. Leaf prints can be made with acrylic paints, a brush, an art roller (brayer), and paper. If you don't have a brayer, use a rolling pin or a large spoon. **(a)** Paint the leaf's underside (where the structure is more pronounced) and place it paint-down on paper. **(b)** Cover with a folded sheet of newspaper or paper towel and firmly roll (or rub with the underside of the spoon). **(c)** Keep the painted leaves and watch how they change as they dry.

All these techniques can be used to decorate presents and to make gift and greeting cards or wall hangings. Combine your artworks into a collage by cutting out the rubbings and/or prints and gluing them onto the stencil picture.

Leaf prints can be made from just about any kind of leaves.

Tips and Tidbits

As they absorb carbon dioxide—a major greenhouse (heat-trapping) gas that contributes to global warming—leaves also help filter out impurities in the air. A healthy tree can absorb 13 to 26 pounds of CO^2 gas a year.

A large maple tree may have about 500,000 leaves.

Trees with leaves help muffle noise. Even without their leaves, trees reduce noise, just not as well.

To preserve leaves in a collection (and make them easier to print from), press the leaves between wax paper, newspaper, or cardboard weighted with a stack of heavy books for two or three days. Or put a leaf between two sheets of wax paper covered (on both sides) by newspaper and iron them at low heat setting.

Leaves lose their green color when gradual changes in the weather and the amount of sunlight cut off chlorophyll production. As existing green chlorophyll breaks down, other colors in the leaf begin to show through.

Create a leaf skeleton. Simmer several leaves over low heat for half an hour. Put them in a bucket of water for a few weeks. Change the water if it starts to smell after a while. As the green part rots away, the more durable, veinlike skeleton remains. Rinse the leaf skeletons, dry them, and add them to your Treebook.

Start a leaf scrapbook, with pressed leaves glued to the pages. Instead of glue, you can protect the leaves with clear, self-sticking paper, available at art supply stores. Identify each with the name of the tree.

Evergreen leaves—usually needles, but not always—are covered with a waxlike substance that protects them from freezing temperatures. Holly, live oak, and palm trees are three evergreens with nonneedle leaves.

Evergreens also lose their leaves, but, unlike deciduous trees, they do it gradually and continuously. Each needle may remain on the tree for about two to four years.

MAKE TWIG WHISTLES

LEVEL: Naturalist (medium; about 1 hour)

SEASONS: All

MATERIALS:

Twigs from ailanthus, or other soft-core trees, at least 6" long, ½" diameter, and fairly straight (the larger the twig, the deeper the sound)
Brace and bit, power drill, or hand drill, with bits about ¼" smaller than the twig's diameter
Coping saw or hacksaw
Sharp knife (Exacto, or wood-cutting tools)
Balsa, cork, or other soft wood
White glue

INTRODUCTION

Wooden instruments are just a few of many tree products that enrich our lives. Among the oldest is the wood whistle.

Choice of wood is critical—look for hollow branches or those with a soft inner core. The ailanthus, also known as "tree of heaven," is a good choice. Its wood is soft, with a spongy inner core, and the trees are abundant—they often can be found growing in vacant city lots. If you can't find an ailanthus, try elderberry twigs, willow branches, squash leaf stems, or bamboo.

Practiced young whittlers will be able to accomplish most of these cutting tasks, but newcomers to woodworking may only be able to help with selecting a twig, gluing the mouthpiece plug, and general consulting, such as choosing the location for the holes and the shape of the mouthpiece.

If your first effort doesn't sound so good, don't despair—they get easier with practice. After you've become a gifted pipe-maker, you can elaborate and embellish to your heart's content.

STEPS

1. Choose your sticks early and allow them to dry for a few weeks to make the core easier to remove. This also reduces the water content and shrinkage, but it makes the wood more brittle.
2. Hollow out your branch. This can be done using a drill, rat-tailed rasp/file, or even a stick, if the core is soft enough. When you cut your ailanthus twig, you may have noticed a peculiar odor. Although unpleasant odor sometimes warns of toxicity, ailanthus is not poisonous. The fresh-cut wood *does* taste unpleasant, which is another good reason to dry it before you begin work.
3. Cut the mouthpiece to resemble that of a recorder (the instrument, a type of fipple flute).
4. Cut a notch about an inch from the tip of the mouthpiece and a third of the way into the whistle. The angle should be about 45 degrees.
5. Cut and sand a piece of balsa wood (or other soft wood, such as cork) to fit into the mouthpiece. It should be about an inch long—reaching from the tip of the mouthpiece to the beginning of the notch. Make it flat on top, with a slight upward slant.
6. Insert the plug with the flat side up, inclining upward toward the notch.
7. Test the whistle. For smaller pipes, plug the end with your finger. Longer instruments (10 inches or more) generally don't require this. You may need to adjust the slant of the mouthpiece plug for optimal sound.
8. Glue the mouthpiece into place and let it dry.
9. Trim the plug to fit the mouthpiece.
10. Now you have a choice to make. Plug the end for a single-toned whistle, or make it multitonal. For a multitoned whistle, drill a few holes through the top—about an inch from the notch

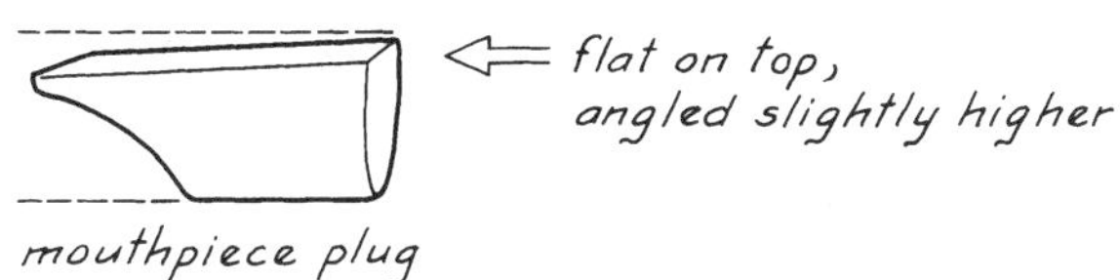

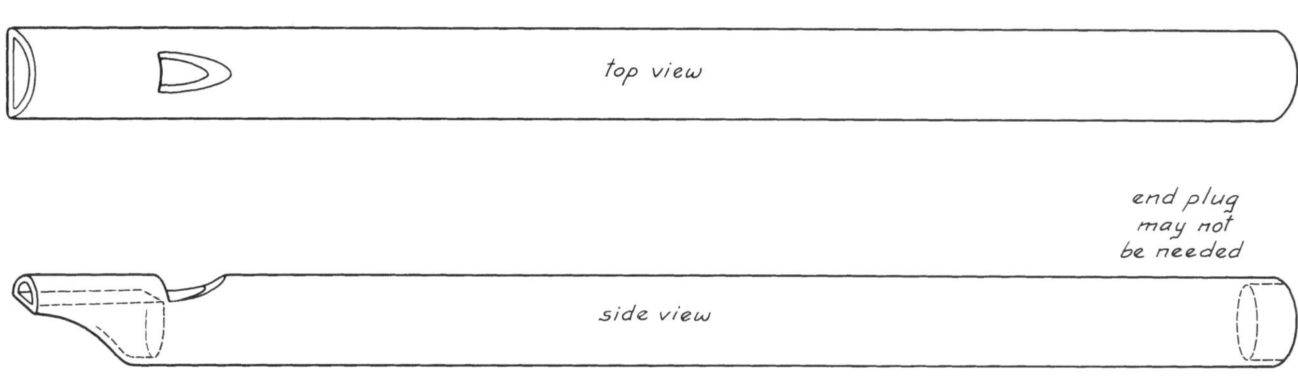

Diagram of a twig whistle

and an inch or so apart—and then plug the end and create a recorder-like instrument.

11. Decorate your pipes with carvings, paint, or other embellishments. The natural look is also nice.

Finished whistles in many shapes and sizes

Find Out More

See Bart Hopkin, *Making Simple Musical Instruments* (Asheville, NC: Lark Books, 1995).

Tips and Tidbits

Tie three or more single-toned pipes together in descending size to make a multitoned instrument similar to a panpipe.

Make loopy slide whistles by tying cotton covered by a piece of cloth to a chopstick, dowel, or other thin stick, so it fits snugly but still slides easily in the end of the whistle.

Lunch on a Limb

LEVEL: Pathfinder (low; about 1 hour)

SEASONS: Spring, summer, fall, and mild winter

MATERIALS:

Picnic lunch (with tree products such as fruits and nuts)

Book bag, small backpack, or shoulder bag

OPTIONAL

Rope

Magnifying glass

INTRODUCTION

Consider the limbs of a tree. They extend outward from the trunk, often at unlikely angles. Filled with waterlogged wood and tipped by wind-catching leaves, it's a wonder they don't start drooping after a few years, or centuries.

Trees are nature's furniture and jungle gyms. They are a child's proving ground and secret place. They offer many climbers their first "bird's-eye view" of the world—an entirely new perspective. But tree-climbing is not just a child's domain—or at least, it shouldn't be. When was the last time you spent some time in a tree with your feet dangling in the breeze?

STEPS

1. Some balmy day, when your unsuspecting offspring are bored to tears, suggest a picnic, but don't say where.
2. Secretly choose a sturdy and accessible climbing tree for this activity. Your adoptive tree might be a good candidate (see Adopt a Tree activities, page 76).
3. Pack your edible goodies (and a magnifying glass) in a book bag or such.
4. Troop out to the tree of choice, look around, and announce: "This looks like a good place."
5. If it's a maple tree and the season is right, gather some helicopter seeds for postlunch launch.
6. Boost your youngsters up, and have them pull up the lunch bag on a rope. Or, strap the bag on your back and follow them up. Find a comfortable height for everyone, unpack the goodies, and enjoy the simple pleasures of lunch on a limb. If climbing is out of the question, park yourselves under the tree, and go from there.

Life in a Tree

Make good use of your senses while sitting in or beneath your tree. Smell the air, feel the bark, taste the wholesome fruits and nuts that you brought along, listen to the rustling leaves, look for insects and other visitors—some of them will be looking for lunch, as well.

Try acting like a bird or squirrel and see if your companions follow the lead. Watch the seeds pinwheel to the ground. Imagine how life would be different if we all lived in trees instead of houses. It's easy to spend an hour or more in a good climbing tree.

Take the Next Step

Back on solid ground, have the kids close their eyes and imagine their feet turning into roots. Legs and torsos slowly become gnarly tree trunks, arms become limbs, fingers turn to leafy twigs. Feel the water flow from the ground, into your roots, through your trunk and branches, and out again through your leaves. Soak up life-giving sun and feel yourself grow stronger, taller.

Imagine a storm brewing, striking with rain and lightning, and leaving behind a soothing calm. Some of the birds that sought shelter in your arms remain to rest or to feed on insects, while others twitter and dart away, continuing their search for mates and nesting places.

If a tree could talk, what stories would it tell us?

Find Out More

See Judy Braus, ed., *Ranger Rick's NatureScope: Trees Are Terrific* (Vienna, VA: National Wildlife Federation, 1992).

Tips and Tidbits

Tree seeds spread in many ways. Some are covered by fruit that is eaten, some fly with the wind, some roll, or are squirreled away by small animals. Can you think of other ways tree seeds get around?

List all the things in one room that are made from trees or tree products. Some items you might not think of include cork, cellophane, many foods and spices, rubber bands, soap, and turpentine.

If you listen closely on a still day, you can sometimes hear water moving inside the tree. Try this in spring or early summer, when the tree's juices are flowing at full force. On smooth-barked trees, a stethoscope can help. When trees are flowering, they sometimes sound like beehives, swarming with pollen-gathering bees.

Every state has an official tree. If you don't already know yours, find out.

Almost a third of the world's land area is covered by trees.

The world's oldest trees are bristlecone pines, which can live to be more than 4,000 years old. They grow in the southwestern United States. The world's tallest trees are California redwoods, which can grow higher than 350 feet, more than 80 feet in circumference, and with bark as thick as 2 feet. One 272-foot redwood weighs an estimated 12 million pounds.

PART III

Beyond Your Backyard—Going Farther Afield

Creeks, Streams, and Rivers

ADOPT A WATERWAY

Trash floating in the Anacostia River, in Washington, DC

LEVEL: Pathfinder (low; time required depends on waterway)

SEASONS: Spring, summer, fall, and mild winter

MATERIALS:
Camera
Detailed map (county, region, or state)
Adoption certificate
Materials for a Farther Afield Album (see **Take the Next Step,** below)

INTRODUCTION

When someone pours paint thinner or automotive oil down a storm drain, where does it go? Too often, it flows through the sewer and into a small creek, stream, or river.

These so-called minor waterways are all part of the earth's gravity-driven plumbing system, which constantly recycles and purifies our limited supply of freshwater. Minor waterways empty into larger waterways, which eventually flow into still larger waterways, such as estuaries, gulfs, seas, and oceans. Some also help replenish our drinking-water reservoirs.

As lesser elements of a much greater whole, creeks, streams, and small rivers are not always given the respect they deserve. We dump trash and sewage into them, polluting the water. We cut trees and shrubs along their banks. Erosion follows, filling the water and bed with sediment, which buries plant life or prevents it from absorbing enough light to survive. Water flow—the speed and/or volume—changes and, in some cases, ceases entirely. The water's average temperature may rise or drop. As conditions deteriorate, aquatic organisms and the creatures that depend on them begin to disappear or relocate.

Small as they are, these waterways are critical to the health of the local, regional, and worldwide water cycle. They are a first line of defense in efforts to keep our water clean. Adopt a nearby waterway not only to be on the front lines of pollution control, but to learn about waterways and how to keep them healthy.

STEPS

1. Choose a small section of a nearby minor

waterway to adopt and visit about once a month. Try to find one with trashy banks or one that otherwise seems to need some help.

2. Take pictures of the stream, both the attractive and the unattractive aspects.
3. Locate it on a map, to see where it originates, what larger waterways it empties into, and where those waters eventually flow.
4. Take get-to-know-you hikes alongside.
5. As with your adopted backyard tree (see activity on page 76), make an official certificate with the date of adoption and the waterway's name.
6. Look for places where pipes drain into the water. Does the water look and smell clean? Is the surrounding plant life as healthy as elsewhere? If it looks and/or smells polluted, it probably is. Of course, pollution doesn't always look or smell bad. Find out who owns the other end of the pipe and whether it is a legal outlet.

A small stream runs brown with sediment immediately after a heavy rain.

Long Term

If you get to the point where your section of the waterway is clear of trash and doesn't need monthly visits, expand your sphere of influence to include a larger section of the waterway or a small part of another one. Organize a cleanup crew to collect trash in and around the water once or twice a year. Are there places that could use some trees? Work with local government and property owners to collect money for trees and plant them along the banks.

Be sure to spend some time just enjoying the sound and beauty of your waterway as well.

Take the Next Step

Continue to take pictures of your adopted waterway over the course of a year. Collect these photos along with written impressions and accounts of your visits (including weather conditions) in an album, much like the Backyard Habitat Album described in the first part of this book. This can be the beginning of a personal Farther Afield Album, documenting your activities and explorations beyond the backyard. Together with the Backyard Habitat Album, it should help you gain a greater understanding of how your backyard and surrounding areas are interrelated.

Find Out More

For information about organized Adopt a Stream programs, see the **Resources** listing, page 126.

Tips and Tidbits

Be careful around waterways. Banks and rocks may be slippery, and the water may be swifter, deeper, or colder than you think. If you wade in, always wear thick-soled boots or tennis shoes as protection from rusty metal or broken glass.

A watershed includes all land and the water that flows over it toward a common destination. Most of this water flows (drains) into creeks, streams, rivers, ponds, lakes, wetlands, and oceans. The Mississippi River watershed drains more than a million square miles, almost half the area of the United States.

Digging a hole and pouring oil or other pollutants into it is no better than pouring it down a storm drain. Pollutants in the ground will likely end up in the groundwater that flows under the surface and eventually feeds a stream or other waterway.

Every year, people pull thousands of pounds of trash from America's waterways. One group working for two months in 1992 removed 3,000 tires, 12 bicycles, 7 shopping carts, 2 engine blocks, and several car batteries from a 3-mile section of a creek near Washington, DC.

About 16 trillion gallons of sewage and industrial waste are dumped into American rivers and coastal waters every year. By comparison, about 400 trillion gallons of rainwater fall in the United States during an average year.

Nearly three-quarters of the earth's surface is covered by water. Of all the world's water, only about 3 percent is freshwater. Of that, nearly 80 percent is frozen in glaciers, icebergs, and icecaps. That leaves us with less than 1 percent of the planet's water, and much of that is beyond our reach or polluted.

RACING WATERS

LEVEL: Pathfinder/Naturalist (low/medium; about 2 hours)

SEASONS: Spring, summer, and fall

MATERIALS:

Twigs, branches, and/or bark
Orange or lemon
Vines
Leaves
Tape measure or yardstick
Twine (for start and finish lines)
Watch with second hand or a stopwatch
Pencil or pen
Paper (for recording measurements and observations)
Graph paper

INTRODUCTION

Water volume and speed are critical to the health of a waterway and to that of its inhabitants. Of course, seasonal changes affect the flow, but organisms that depend on the water have developed adaptations to survive natural fluctuations. During temporary dry spells, for instance, crayfish and other creatures can remain moist in deep burrows. Unnatural, long-term changes, however, can permanently disrupt stream life.

Familiarize yourself with your waterway's flow by measuring its water velocity and volume. Take as many other measurements as you can to create a profile.

STEPS

1. Collect sticks, fallen bark, and vines (or use twine) to construct small rafts to race on your waterway. Incorporate a mast with a leaf as a sail, if you want to.
2. Measure a 10-foot stretch of your waterway and construct a start and finish line.
3. Count the seconds it takes your boats to travel 10 feet.
4. Divide 10 by the number of seconds counted to determine the water's velocity in feet per second.
   10 ft. ÷ ______ sec. = ______ ft./sec.
   (distance) (time) (velocity)
5. Repeat several times to get an average velocity for the segment.
6. Now repeat the experiment using an orange or lemon (if the waterway is deep enough) or remove the sail and use your raft or boat.
7. Compare these measurements with each other and with the velocity of other sections. In some streams the submerged fruit method is more accurate, because anything floating on the surface may be influenced by wind or variations in surface speed.

8. If your waterway is not too wide or deep, you can make a rough estimate of its flow (volume). Measure the width at a typical spot.
9. Tie a string with knots or marks every 5 inches and tie it straight across the stream close to water level.
10. Measure the depth at each of the marks. Try to just touch the bed of the waterway with the measuring stick or tape; don't push it down into the sediments, if there are any.
11. Record your measurements and use graph paper to make a cross section, with each square representing 25 square inches.
12. Count the squares to get the square inches of water in the cross section.
13. Multiply velocity by 12 to convert feet per second into inches per second, and multiply that by the cross-section number to get an approximate measure of the volume in cubic inches per second.
14. To get cubic feet per second, divide your volume figure by 1,728.

EXAMPLE: A stream has a velocity of 7 inches per second. A cross-section profile gives an estimated 52 boxes, or 1,300 square inches. Multiply 1,300 by 7 to get 9,100 cubic inches (about 5 cubic feet) of water per second.

Racing rafts is one way to measure a stream's velocity.

____ in./sec. × ____ sq. in. = ____ cubic in./sec.
(velocity) (area) (volume)

Walnut shell Boats and Rafts

You can also use walnut shell halves to make boats and rafts. Use modeling clay or beeswax, toothpicks, and small leaves to make sails in individual shell halves. Glue four half-shells onto the four corners of a thin piece of wood or bark. Use modeling clay or beeswax, a twig, and a large leaf to make a sail. If no walnut shells are handy, use pieces of cork or balsa wood.

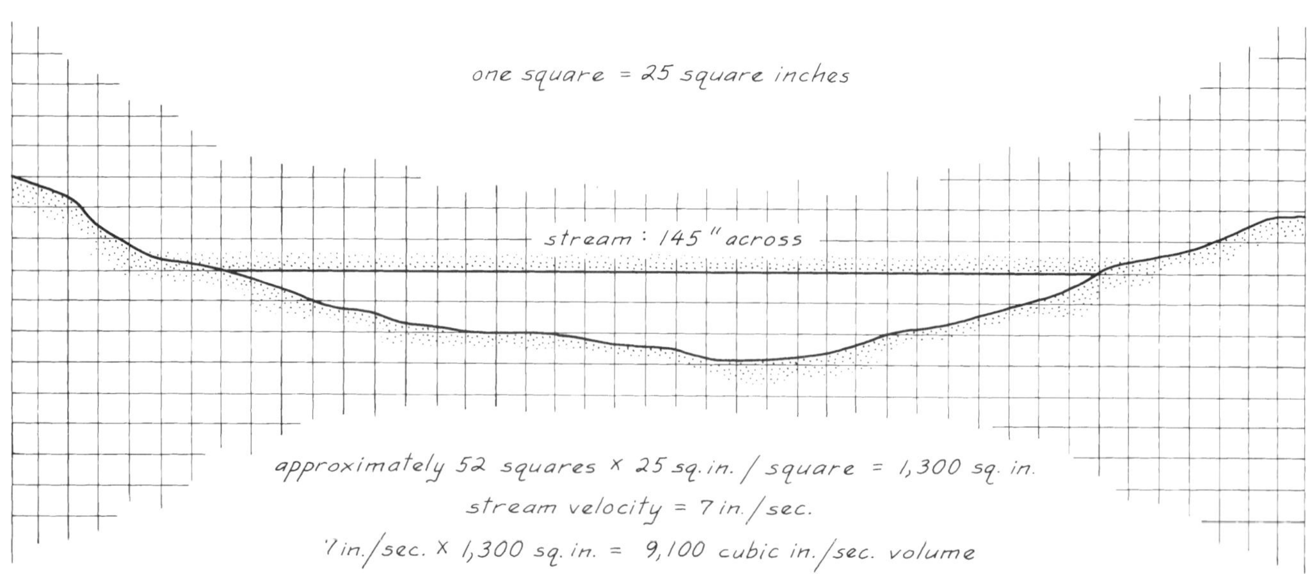

Transfer your measurements to graph paper to create a scale model of a stream profile.

Find Out More

See Joanna Cole, *The Magic School Bus at the Waterworks* (New York: Scholastic, 1986) (for younger readers).

Also see the **Resources** listing, page 127.

Tips and Tidbits

Moving water in streams contains more oxygen than still water in most ponds and lakes. The water's motion also stirs up nutrients for animals to feed upon.

Algae is the main source of food from plants in a stream.

The Amazon, which has the greatest flow of any river in the world, disgorges some 50 million gallons of water per second into the Atlantic Ocean.

The Mississippi, with the greatest flow of any U.S. river, carries an average of about 5 million gallons per second into the Gulf of Mexico. During rainy seasons, this may increase to more than 17 million gallons per second. Along with the water, about 400 million cubic yards of suspended mud, sand, and other materials are deposited into the delta and gulf every year.

Measuring a stream's width and its depth in several places will help you map its profile.

Take a Streamside Creature Survey

LEVEL: Naturalist (medium; about 2 hours)

SEASONS: Late spring, summer, and early fall

MATERIALS:

Collection containers (clear plastic bottles or bags; glass is not recommended)
Aquarium net (to make your own, see activity on page 97)
Proper attire: boots, long pants, and long-sleeved shirt
Magnifying glass
Paper and pen or pencil

OPTIONAL

Field guide to river and stream wildlife (see below)

INTRODUCTION

The presence of plants and animals in and around a waterway is a good indicator of its health. In general, when water quality declines, not all species are affected the same way. Some creatures are more hardy; they can survive all but the most drastic changes. Other species are more sensitive; these are usually the first to be affected by changing conditions. Because they act as an early warning system, these sensitive creatures are called indicator species.

Acquaint yourself with the animal life in your

adopted waterway section by spending a few hours looking for them. A survey is simply a written list of the animals in a habitat. A complete scientific survey is a very thorough attempt to locate and identify every species, and it requires much more time. For this activity, you can't expect to find every inhabitant of your waterway, but if you make repeated visits and know what to look for, you might eventually get to know most of them.

STEPS

1. Turn over stones and scrape the undersides; use a stick to dig or poke around in the bottom of the waterway.
2. In addition to active searching, be sure to remain very still while you watch a pool or other small area. Sometimes, if you wait long enough without moving, aquatic animals will come out of hiding.
3. Don't look just for live animals, also look for their signs. These include tracks, shells, bones, burrows, and any other indications of animal activity.
4. If you can't bring along a field guide, make sketches of your finds and try to identify the drawings at home.

Crayfish

Among the animals most commonly found in and around healthy streams are crayfish, also known as crawdads. These crustaceans, which grow to be about 4 inches long, are close relatives of much larger saltwater lobsters. Some species of crayfish burrow into the soil along streams, making tunnels that typically have both under- and above-water openings. Around their above-water openings, some species build muddy towers that can be several inches tall.

These relatives of spiders and other arthropods are most active at night, when they scavenge the bottoms for plant matter, worms, insect larva, tadpoles, small fish, and bits of dead animals. Female crayfish carry their black, brown, or greenish eggs under their tails. Even after the young hatch, they may remain clustered in the sheltered security of their mother's tail for several days before venturing off on their own.

To pick up a crayfish underwater, you have to be quick. They use their fanned tail to whisk themselves along backwards. On land, they are slow, but fierce, so watch out for their pinchers. Grasp the crayfish with your thumb and forefinger behind the front pinchers. Crayfish need water with a lot of dissolved oxygen, so if you want to take one home for short-term observation, you will need an aerator or some other way to pump oxygen into the water.

Newt Home

If you find a couple of salamanders or young newts (called efts), you can bring them home for observation. A ventilated terrarium makes a good, moist home for them (when occupied by live animals, a terrarium can also be called a vivarium). Give them a shallow, ground-level dish of fresh water and feed them small earthworms (from your worm bin, if you have one). They may be kept during winter and released in spring where you found them. Don't try to pick them up by the tail, because it may drop off (a new one will eventually grow). Their eggs are laid in clear, jellylike balls attached to underwater vegetation.

This is a small specimen, but the crayfish is North America's largest freshwater crustacean.

Find Out More

See the **Resources** listing, page 127.

Tips and Tidbits

Visit your waterway in the early mornings and afternoons for the best chance of seeing wildlife. Approach quietly, so you don't scare these other visitors away.

Because its temperature changes much more slowly than that of air, water helps protect its inhabitants from drastic temperature fluctuations.

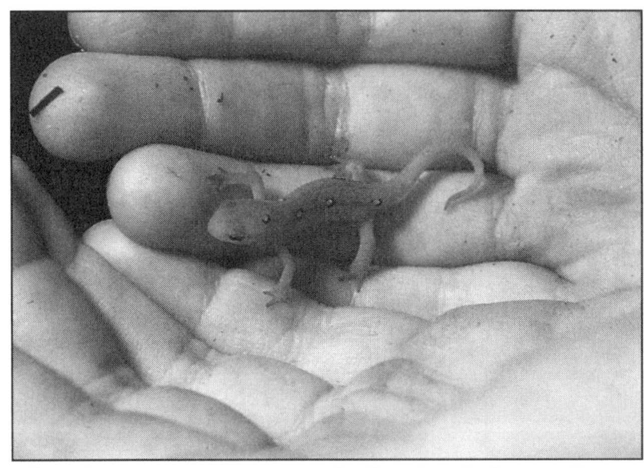

This red eft—a young newt—is only about 3 inches long. Look for efts in the woods after summer rains.

Water striders and minnows are typical residents in creeks, streams, and small rivers.

Watch your step! Algae and other substances clinging to rocks make them slippery.

Water striders have tiny hairs on their legs that allow them to skate on the water's surface. Drop a dead mosquito or other small insect nearby and see if the predatory strider pounces on it.

A clean, 5-gallon paint container with a white, plastic trash-can liner makes an excellent short-term observatory. White jar lids make good pocket-sized observatories. Large spoons and turkey basters are good for picking up small organisms, and one-piece, plastic ice trays help keep them separated.

Ponds and Lakes

MAKE AN UNDERWATER VIEWER

LEVEL: Pathfinder (low; about 15 minutes)

SEASONS: Spring, summer, and fall

MATERIALS:

Coffee or juice can, or a half-gallon milk carton
Plastic wrap
2 or more rubber bands

OPTIONAL

Petroleum jelly
Duct tape

INTRODUCTION

If you look only at the water's surface and surroundings, you miss most of what a pond or lake is about. But it's difficult to see through the reflective surfaces of still waters.

Although the water in most ponds and lakes is murky, enough sunlight penetrates the top 6 inches or so to allow underwater viewing. This top layer of water is critical to life in the pond, because that is where most photosynthesis takes place in the water's phytoplankton—algae and other floating plants that are the most abundant basic food in a typical pond or lake. These are the mainstay for many simple, plant-eating organisms, which in turn become food for larger creatures on up the food chain.

STEPS

1. Cut both ends off a can or milk carton and cover one end with plastic wrap, so that it comes at least halfway up the sides.
2. Gather the plastic wrap so there are no wrinkles in the viewing end and put a rubber band around the bottom. Alternatively, you can use the plastic lid of the coffee can to hold the cellophane at the bottom. Just cut away all but ¼ inch of the inner cover. For the best seal, smear some petroleum jelly around the outer surface of the can's bottom before putting the clear plastic on.
3. Put another rubber band where the plastic ends near the top of the container. Wrap the plastic and rubber band with duct tape for a better seal. Eliminate any wrinkles in the "lens"—they will distort your view.

Underwater viewer in use

4. The viewer can be used from a boat, a low pier, along the water's edge, or while standing in the water. It can also be used in streams (see the waterway activities on pages 87–93). Be extra careful if you lean out over the water or wade into it. If you can, wear hip waders in the water or thin, long pants with an old pair of sneakers or heavy-soled boots. To avoid getting bubbles on the lens, make a habit of putting the viewer in the water at an angle. If your viewer catches some bubbles, just tilt it to the side. Notice that what you see through the viewer is magnified by light passing through the water.

   Don't worry if some water gets in your viewer. You will still be able to see pretty well, as long as water covers the entire plastic lens. However, water inside the can cancels out the viewer's magnification.

FIND OUT MORE

See George K. Reid, *Golden Nature Guide: Pond Life* (New York: Golden Press, 1987) (also helpful in identifying many stream-dwelling organisms).

Tips and Tidbits

Most of the world's available freshwater is held in ponds and lakes. These bodies of water can be deep or shallow, natural or manmade.

It is not always easy to distinguish between lakes and ponds. Lakes are generally deeper than ponds—so deep, in fact, that plants grow only near the shore. Other differences include daily water-temperature and dissolved-oxygen variations, and the amount of wave action on downwind shores.

Most activity in a pond or lake happens in the area called the littoral zone, from the water's edge to where no more rooted plants grow. The width of this zone varies, depending on the depth of the pond or lake, but it contains the greatest number of organisms.

Over time, all ponds and lakes get shallower and shallower until they eventually are filled in. That's because dead plants and animals and suspended dirt from runoff sink to the bottom. As the bottom rises and the water becomes shallower, more plants can take root. The plants not only draw off water, but their stems and roots trap debris and anchor the soil. This process may take decades, centuries, or millennia.

Ponds and lakes have four major habitats: water surface, open water, shoreline, and bottom. Each is home to different communities of organisms, with many creatures using more than one habitat.

As with streams and other moving waterways, still-water ponds and lakes are wildlife magnets. Raccoons, muskrats, weasels, otter, deer, and other mammals visit ponds for water and/or food. Waterbirds may attract eagles and other birds of prey. Osprey hunt the waters for fish. Look for wildlife in the early morning and late afternoon, when it is most active and fewer people are out and about.

Lake Superior is the world's largest freshwater lake.

Make an Aquatic Critter Collector

LEVEL: Pathfinder (low; about 1 hour)

SEASONS: All; for use in spring, summer, and fall

MATERIALS:

Wire coat hanger
Pole (broomstick, 1" dowel, etc.), at least 2' to 4' long
Wood screw (flat- or roundheaded, washer optional)
Screwdriver
Drill and bit (for pilot hole)
Pliers
Duct tape
Stocking or pantyhose (or nylon net from a fabric shop)
Scissors
Needle and thread, yarn, or nylon string

OPTIONAL
Strip of cloth, 3" wide and as long as the wire loop

INTRODUCTION

Few larger animal species in a pond or lake eat algae, at least not on purpose. But they do eat many of the tiny, plant-eating animals that feed on algae as well as the smaller animals that feed on those algae eaters.

Even the smallest insect nymphs, bottom-dwelling worms, and snails eventually become food for other animals in the food web, or they die, and their bodies decay, returning nutrients to the ecosystem. Without these smaller organisms, larger animals could not survive in the pond.

To observe these creatures, you first have to find and catch them. You can buy collection tools from aquarium supply stores and some hobby or science shops, but it's much less expensive to make them

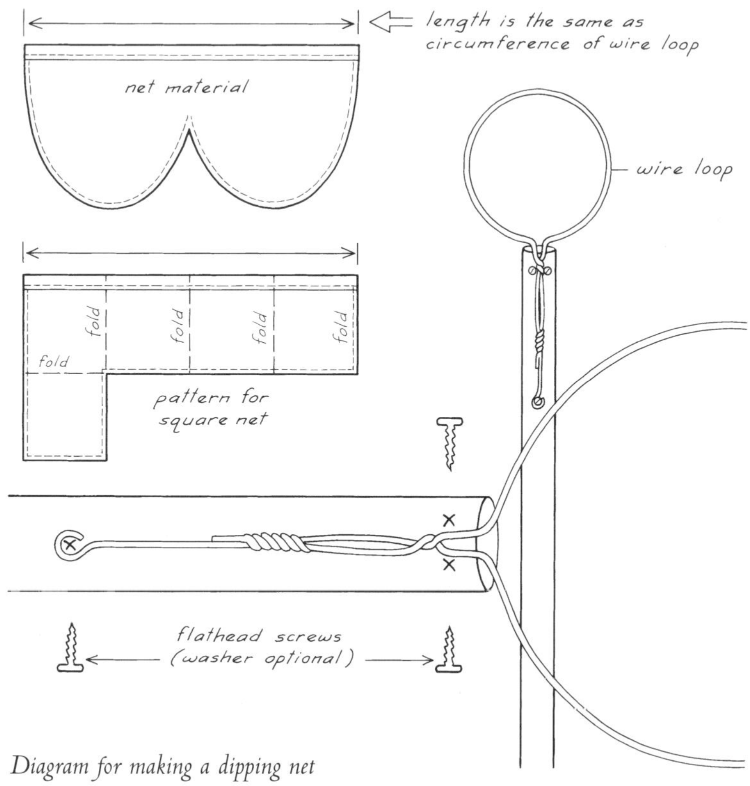

Diagram for making a dipping net

yourself. Many of these collection tools can be used in rivers and streams as well.

STEPS

1. Bend the hanger into a roughly circular or rectangular shape. Don't make the opening too large, or you may not be able to fit the stocking around the wire loop.
2. Straighten the curved hanger and make a small loop at the end.
3. Lay this end against the pole, so that the net opening is at the end of the pole and the wire lies flat against the wood.
4. Mark the point inside the small loop and drill a pilot hole.
5. Drive a screw (with a washer, for extra hold) to secure the loop.
6. At the end of the pole, drill holes on either side of the joined wires and drive a screw in each hole.

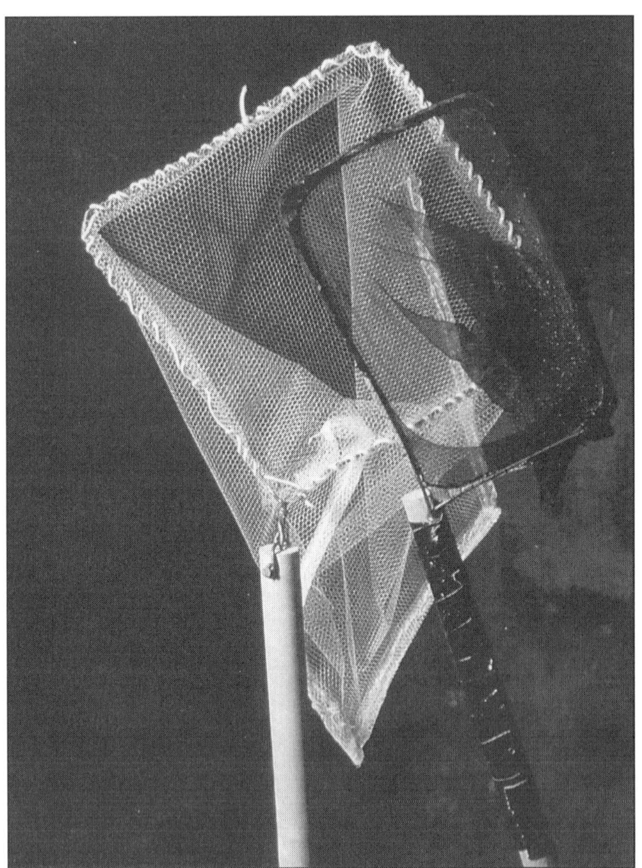

Finished nets

Dipping net in use

7. Wrap the entire end with duct tape.
8. If the stockings or pantyhose are reinforced at the top, use that part to attach the net to the loop. Stretch the nylon around the loop with the end on the outside.
9. Use needle, thread, and a wraparound stitch to sew the nylon to the loop. For a stronger net, fold a 3-inch-wide strip of fabric over the entire loop and sew it on, or cover the wire with folded-over duct tape.
10. Shorten the stocking to no more than a foot long by folding it and sewing an end seam.
11. Cut off the extra nylon, and your net is ready for use. It may seem short, but under water it will stretch somewhat. This tool also can be used as an insect net.

Nylon Net Method

You're not out of luck if you can't scrounge up an old stocking. Cut nylon net into a rounded W shape, with the straight distance between the two ends equal to the circumference of the wire loop. Attach your protective 3-inch-wide strip, then sew the net together and sew it onto the wire loop. This net-making method has advantages over using stockings or pantyhose: not only will the net not run, but you don't stretch it around the loop, so the inside area is larger. The only disadvantage (other than requiring more work) is that the net may not be as fine-meshed as stocking material.

Find Out More

See the **Resources** listing, page 127.

Tips and Tidbits

No stockings or sewing skills? Use duct tape to fasten an old, hand-held strainer to a pole.

One way to use the net is to stir up the bottom with a stick or your well-protected feet and use the net to collect the creatures that get stirred up.

When you go netting, take along a large, preferably white, pail, or a clear container to fill partway with water from the pond or lake. Empty your net into the container for observation. You also can use a white trash bag as a container lining.

Another easy-to-make collection tool—called a seine or kick net—can be made from plastic window screen or net stapled to two 4-foot-long segments of 1 × 2-inch wood (broomsticks, poles, etc.). Small versions can be operated by one person; larger ones are intended for use by two people.

About 5,000 species of North American insects spend at least part of their lives in water.

The absence of certain organisms in a body of water can provide clues to whether the water is polluted. Sludge worms can live in even very polluted waters; the nymphs of several species of caddisflies, stoneflies, and mayflies can't. Pike and some other fish can't live in oxygen-poor water, but carp and perch can.

Hunt for Amphibian Eggs

LEVEL: Pathfinder (low; about 1 hour)

SEASONS: Spring (also late winter and summer in some regions)

MATERIALS:
Underwater viewer (see activity, page 95)
Aquatic Critter Collector (see activity, page 97)
Bucket or jar
Waders, muckabout boots, or shoes

OPTIONAL
Pond-life guidebook
Thermometer
Notebook and pen or pencil
Nylon string and small bits of meat
Powerful flashlight

INTRODUCTION

America's largest frog, the bullfrog, is one of the most common large residents of ponds and lakes. Found throughout most of the eastern and central United States, it can grow to be 8 inches long (plus 10-inch-long legs). Bullfrogs eat insects and other small creatures, but they also have been known to catch and eat small birds and even baby alligators. They breed and lay eggs in late winter or early spring. The jellylike egg masses are usually attached to underwater vegetation. Tadpoles hatch in about six days and can be 4 to 6 inches long and take two years to develop into adults.

Tiger salamanders and newts are two of the most common small amphibians found around lakes and ponds. The tigers are the largest land-dwelling salamander species in the world, reaching 6 to 13 inches long. They lay egg masses on underwater debris starting in late winter and continuing through the summer in southern regions.

Eastern newts breed from late winter to early spring and lay several hundred eggs on underwater vegetation. Incubation takes three to eight weeks. Larval newts begin life breathing through exterior gills, which they lose after a year when they become

A tadpole jar should have algae and water plants for the tadpoles to eat.

lung-breathing, bright reddish- or orange-colored efts. They then leave the water and live in surrounding woods for one to three years, after which they remain in and around ponds or streams as adults.

STEPS

1. Use nets and/or dippers to find eggs from frogs, toads, newts, salamanders, or other amphibians. Don't take all the eggs you find, but just a portion.
2. If possible, measure the temperature of the water where you find them.
3. Bring the eggs home and keep them in a jar or aquarium.
4. If you measured the temperature where you found the eggs, try to find a spot indoors where the water temperature will be close to your measurement. The container should not be placed in direct sun (unless you want to cook the eggs).
5. Observe the eggs every day as they develop.
6. When replacing evaporated water, use only spring water, pond water, or tap water that has been set out for at least a day. Water should just cover the eggs.
7. When they hatch, observe them for a few days and then return them to the area where you found them.
8. If you want to try to keep some of the young a while longer, return all but a half dozen or so.
9. Add algae and other water plants in your container to provide food and oxygen for the larvae.
10. After about five weeks, the young will need high-protein food, such as the insect larvae they would normally eat. Feed them cheese or bits of meat. Unless you can keep them supplied with food, now is a good time to return your temporary pets to the wild.

Ordering Eggs

Even if you can't find any amphibian eggs, you can order them from a scientific supply store, such as Carolina Biological Supply (see the Observatory listing, page 126 in the **Resources** section). Their shipments of frog or salamander eggs come with an instruction booklet, *Reptiles and Amphibians: Care and Culture.*

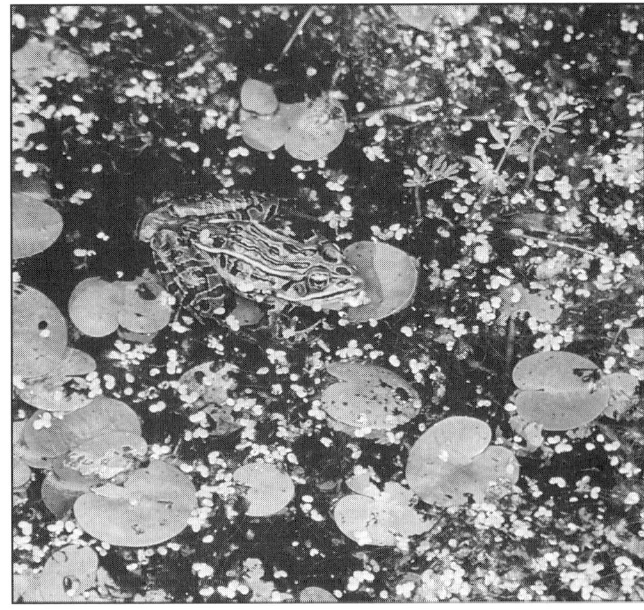

The leopard frog is a common resident in many ponds and lakes in North America.

Related Activities

Try hookless fishing—tie a small piece of meat to a nylon string, put it in the water, and tie the other end to a stick planted in the ground. Sit very still or leave for a half-hour and come back again to check on your lure. Hookless fishing can be even more fun at night, using a powerful flashlight to see what's nibbling at the bait.

Adopt a pond or lake and add it to your Farther Afield Album.

Find Out More

See Karen Dawe, *The Pond Book and Tadpole Tank* (New York: Workman Publishing Co., 1995) (for ages eight and older).

Tips and Tidbits

The life cycle of some amphibians resembles that of many insects in that after they hatch from eggs, they pass through a larval stage before becoming adults.

Not all adult amphibians have lungs. Some breathe only through their moist skin. Even those with lungs also breathe through their skin.

In addition to bullfrogs, other commonly found species around ponds, lakes, and marshes include the green, northern cricket, and leopard frogs.

Visit a pond or lake some moonlit night. Take a powerful flashlight along. When you arrive, listen to the music of the residents for a while in the dark. Then use the flashlight to try to spot frogs and other creatures. Their eyes will reflect the light with an eerie glow.

Swamps and Other Wet Wonderlands

Get Your Feet Wet

LEVEL: Explorer (high; at least 2 hours)

SEASONS: All, weather permitting

MATERIALS:

Protective clothing, such as long pants, long-sleeved shirt, and boots or other sturdy footwear
Underwater viewer (see activity, page 95) and/or collecting equipment

OPTIONAL
Binoculars
Pencil or pen and paper

One of the best ways to see Everglades National Park is from a canoe.

INTRODUCTION

Wetlands can be defined as any inland or coastal area other than ponds, lakes, rivers, and streams, where the (usually) shallow water is the most important influence on the associated plant and animal life. Quite a mouthful. But wetlands are much more than that.

Freshwater wetlands provide food and habitat for many animals. In fact, North American waterfowl migrate along corridors—called flyways—that are dotted by wetlands and other waterways. This is no coincidence. The birds need the refuge and food found in these rich habitats for nesting and resting during migrations that may cover thousands of miles.

In addition to providing habitat for waterfowl and other wildlife, wetlands provide humans with flood and erosion control, water purification, groundwater replenishment, and food, among other benefits.

Explore a wetland in your area and see whether one of the important, protected wetlands in the list below is close enough to visit. Because of climates, migrations, and mosquito populations, some of them are best visited in spring, fall, or winter. The worst season to visit most North American wetlands is in summer.

STEPS

Unless you can fly, the best way to get a feel for shallow wetlands is to wade in. For deeper wetlands, a

In shallow wetlands, including parts of Everglades National Park, you can slog through the slough (pronounced slew*) under the guidance of a park ranger.*

canoe, kayak, or flat-bottomed boat is best. Of course, not all wetlands are suitable for this type of investigation, which should be led by someone who is intimately familiar with the area. At some protected wetlands—such as Everglades National Park—visitors can accompany a naturalist on wading tours, canoe trips, or other educational trips.

In the Everglades, visitors can slog through a slough (pronounced *slew*), which is a wide, shallow trough of slow-moving water. These adventures are especially exciting because you are waist-deep in the same waters that alligators use.

Swamps and marshes can be difficult for the novice to appreciate. Take your time. Go with a knowledgeable guide or bring along a good guidebook. Be sure to call ahead for information on facilities, tours, boat rentals, and best seasons for visiting.

Freshwater Wetlands

The following is a sampling of some of the country's unique and fascinating freshwater wetlands.

STATE	NAME
AK	Yukon Flats National Wildlife Refuge
FL	Everglades National Park
	Big Cypress National Preserve
CA	Tule Lake
GA	Okefenokee Swamp National Wildlife Refuge and Wilderness Area
LA	Rockefeller, Sabine, and Delta National Wildlife Refuges
MN	Agassiz National Wildlife Refuge
IA, MN, MT, ND, SD, WI & Canada	Prairie pothole region
NE	Crescent Lake Wildlife Refuge
NJ	Great Swamp National Wildlife Refuge
NY	Montezuma National Wildlife Refuge
SC	Audubon Sanctuary at Four Holes Swamp, Francis Beidler Forest
TX	Big Thicket National Preserve
VA	Great Dismal Swamp

Find Out More

See William A. Niering, *The Audubon Society Nature Guides: Wetlands* (New York: Alfred A. Knopf, 1985).

See also the **Resources** listing, page 127.

Tips and Tidbits

Never explore a wetland alone—you might disappear into a sinkhole or other underwater trap. Bogs can be especially dangerous. Also, do not collect any plants from these fragile ecosystems.

Wetlands are North America's most productive ecosystems. Estuaries—which are saltwater wetlands—are so productive, they sometimes are compared to tropical rain forests. Some freshwater wetlands are believed to be at least as productive as estuaries.

Hundreds of animals use wetlands, including almost all of the fish and shellfish that we eat. In fact, studies of one wetland found that nearly 700 different species use it.

Wetlands in the lower 48 states account for only about 5 percent of U.S. lands.

In America's Colonial days, people considered marshes and swamps to be dangerous, disease-breeding wastelands. George Washington worked to drain parts of the Great Dismal Swamp in Virginia and North Carolina. He wanted to harvest the timber and turn the area into productive farmland. Today, most of the swamp's remaining acreage is protected as a national wildlife refuge.

The prairie pothole region in the United States and south-central Canada covers about 300,000 square miles and is the continent's most important waterfowl nesting area. Millions of ducks—about half of America's duck population—use the area. For this reason, it is sometimes called a duck factory.

CREATE A WETLAND MODEL

LEVEL: Naturalist (medium; about 1 hour)

SEASONS: All

MATERIALS:
Modeling clay (green, if possible)
Roasting pan
Thick carpet or indoor-outdoor carpet

OPTIONAL
Florist's foam
Cotton swabs
Cotton balls
Toothpicks
Natural materials (pine needles, twigs, grass, etc.)
Paint or colored markers

INTRODUCTION

Wetlands are natural water-purification systems. They slow the motion of faster-flowing rivers and streams, allowing floating particles (sediments) to sink. This buffer action not only removes silt and other particles, it reduces erosion and flooding.

In addition, wetland water is filled with nutrient-devouring bacteria and plants that absorb impurities. In fact, several American communities use a combination of ponds and wetlands to treat their wastewater. Some of these treatment systems produce water that exceeds state and federal purity requirements at much lower cost than modern sewage-treatment facilities.

The water in some wetlands is surprisingly clear.

Explore some aspects of how wetlands work by making a model.

STEPS

(The following is adapted from *Ranger Rick's NatureScope: Wading into Wetlands;* see **Find Out More.**)

1. Mold the clay into a gradual slope reaching from one edge of the roasting pan to the middle.
2. Press the clay firmly against the pan around the edges to prevent seepage. The clay represents the land surrounding a marsh. You can create streams and rivers to channel water into the wetland. Of course, water would also flow under-

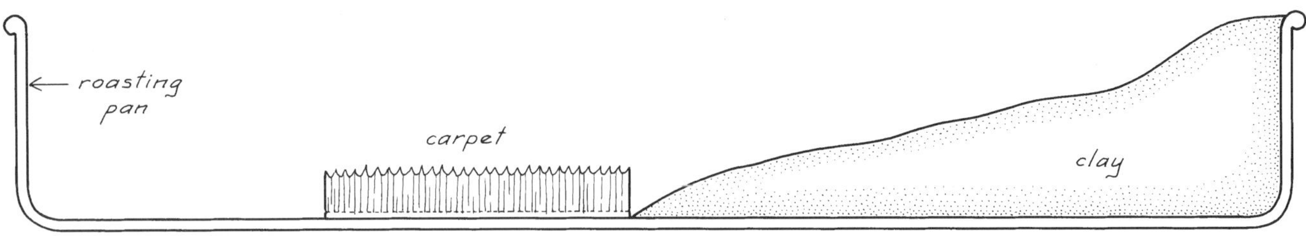

Wetland model

ground in real life, but for the purposes of this experiment, all water flows above ground.

3. Cut a 3-inch-wide piece of carpet to fit snugly against the edge of the clay and the sides of the pan. This represents a wetland. The open area represents a lake, river, or ocean that receives water from the wetland.
4. To demonstrate a wetland's flood-controlling properties, moisten the carpet and pour off any excess water.
5. Slowly pour water onto the land and note how long it takes to come out of the marsh. Without the carpet, the water would flow directly into the river, lake, or other water body.
6. Investigate a wetland's water purification properties by repeating the experiment using muddy water in a clear container. Pour only about half of the muddy water into the model.
7. Pour the water that passed through the marsh into another clear container and compare the two. The wetland water should be noticeably clearer than the water in the original container.
8. Wetlands can't be expected to do it all, though. Rinse the carpet and try the experiment using food coloring in the water. The dye represents pollution such as gasoline or oil that a wetland can't purify.
9. As a final activity, replace the carpet with a 1-inch-thick strip of florist's foam. The foam can fill the entire half of the pan or taper off into a watery area (represented by plastic wrap, or colored paper). Make twig trees with colored cotton-ball canopies, pine-needle reeds, cotton-swab cattails, and so forth. Now you have a permanent wetland model and a reminder of the importance of wetlands.

Find Out More

See Judy Braus, ed., *Ranger Rick's NatureScope: Wading into Wetlands* (Washington, DC: National Wildlife Federation, 1989).

See also the **Resources** listing, page 128.

Tips and Tidbits

Make a simple water-sample collector. Cut a large hole in the upper half of a plastic milk jug (leave the handle intact). Tie a 6-foot length of strong, nylon string around the handle. Use this to collect water samples beyond your reach. (You may need to put rocks in the bottom to make it sink.)

Fewer than half of America's original 215 million wetland acres in the lower 48 states remain today. Of the remaining wetlands, many are being swallowed by development and agriculture or polluted by man-made contaminants. We are losing nearly 300,000 acres (470 square miles) annually—that's an area nearly half the size of Rhode Island.

More than 20 states have lost half or more of their original wetlands. Iowa and Ohio have lost about 90 percent of theirs.

About half of America's remaining marshes are in Louisiana.

Because of their ability to absorb, hold, and gradually release large quantities of water, wetlands are called nature's sponges.

Forests

Explore Dead Snags and Rotting Logs

LEVEL: Pathfinder (low; about 1 hour)

SEASONS: All

MATERIALS:
Arthropod vacuum (see activity on page 53)
Bugarium (see activity on page 51), or other containers, such as jars and plastic bags
Gardening gloves
Three-pronged gardening tool or hand trowel
White paper, plastic bag, or cloth, at least a few feet square (for sorting organisms)

OPTIONAL
Tree saw (for cross section)
Field guides to invertebrates, fungi, and/or trees
Magnifying glass

INTRODUCTION

If a tree is defined as a tall, wood-stemmed plant with a crown of foliage and a trunk that, when measured at about 5 feet from the ground, has a diameter of 3 inches or more, then a lot of tree growing in one place makes up a forest, right? Hardly.

A forest is a complex system with its own cycles. Just as there are different species of trees, there are many different types of forest: temperate or tropical rain forests, northern coniferous forests, eastern deciduous forests, and southeastern pine forests, among others. Each has different cycles, characteristics, and associated organisms (although there may be much crossover), and within a forest there are many variations, or subhabitats.

One of the best ways to gain a deeper understanding of the complexities of forests is to see how they recycle energy. A whole range of organisms help keep forest cycles working, and an excellent place to see this process in action is in a decaying tree.

Some people consider standing dead trees (snags) and fallen, rotting logs to be wasted wood. Nothing could be further from the truth. In nature, nothing is wasted. These minihabitats provide homes and/or food to numerous organisms, including bacteria, fungi, insects, salamanders, birds, and raccoons. Other plants, such as mosses, ferns, and even tree seedlings often take root in a dead tree. An average-sized tree may take 10 years to fully decay, but a large tree such as a Douglas fir with a 14-foot diameter may take 500 years.

Investigate a standing snag and/or a fallen tree and compare the amount and kinds of life each supports.

STEPS

1. Find a snag and examine it carefully. You may not be able to dig into its wood, but often you can make guesses about what is inside and what animals have used the tree. Rows of small holes are left by a woodpecker. That evidence suggests the presence of grubs, ants, and other woodpecker foods. A large hole or two high up may be home for a woodpecker, an owl, a squirrel,

mice, or other small animals. A hollow snag may house raccoons or opossums, and a large one may be a black bear's winter residence. Look for claw marks on the trunk. Look inside loose bark for the tunnels and paths of bark beetles.

2. When you explore fallen, rotting logs, you'll see that they host a different community of organisms, although there may be some crossover between downed trees and snags. Whereas the outside of a snag tends to be dry most of the time, a fallen log often is a very damp environment. Of course, a fallen log often is in a more advanced state of decay than a snag. But there are other reasons for the difference as well.

   For one, the wood's structure is designed to transport water and sap vertically, from roots to leaves and from leaves to branches, the trunk, and roots. Moisture in a snag gravitates downward. The moisture in a fallen log is held in place longer by the wood's structure. Plus, the underside of a fallen log has a relatively large surface area in contact with the ground. This not only speeds the decay process, but the spongy, decaying wood wicks moisture up into the log, further hastening decay. Fungi in some logs also produce water. Moss or ferns that cover the log will help hold moisture, and their roots help break up the wood.

This common flicker in Florida has made its home in a dead palm tree.

Investigating the life in and around a log

3. Compare the organisms found in logs that are in various stages of decay. Carefully dig into the more decayed logs and spread the rotting litter on a piece of white plastic or cloth for easier sorting.
4. Use a tree saw to cut a cross section of the log.
5. If you can, roll the log over and dig into the ground beneath.
6. When you finish, return the log to its place and cover exposed areas with leaf litter.

It's a fair assumption that the moist environment of a fallen log is home to more organisms than the drier snag, but each provides a niche, and each is critical to forest cycles and the resident animals. That's all in addition to the living trees, which, as seen in the backyard segment on trees, provide wildlife and humans with many benefits.

Find Out More

See George I. Schwartz and Bernice S. Schwartz, *Life in a Log)* Garden City, NY: Natural History Press,

1972) (out of print; look for it in your library).

See also the **Resources** listing, page 128.

Tips and Tidbits

Return to your dead tree every so often to track its progress from forest-floor litter to soil. You may want to make a map and mark your calendar as a reminder.

Because of wood's insulating quality, the temperature inside a dead tree will not fluctuate as widely as that outside. Test this yourself with a thermometer.

To accomplish its recycling work, the forest depends on the F.B.I.—Fungi, Bacteria, and Insects. Together with other organisms, they reduce just about all plant and animal matter to soil.

A forest may seem serene, but a fierce competition is being played out, both above and below ground. Trees compete for sunlight and moisture, forcing them to extend their canopies higher and wider and their roots deeper and wider. Fire, weather, disease, age, pests, competition, and other factors all limit the growth and spread of trees.

SEE DIRT IN THE MAKING

LEVEL: Pathfinder (low; about ½ hour)

SEASONS: All

MATERIALS:

Three-pronged gardening tool, trowel, or shovel
Several sealable plastic sandwich bags or other containers
Light-colored paper, plastic bag, or cloth
Magnifying glass

INTRODUCTION

In a deciduous forest, leaves make up most of the material on the forest floor. You could say that today's leaf litter is tomorrow's soil.

Even within the leaf litter, there are often distinct layers and habitats. The top layer of leaves and branches often is dry, with scarcely any visible organisms or activity. Just below that, the leaves usually are moister and show some signs of decay. As you dig deeper, it gets progressively harder to recognize any leaves at all.

Scratch the surface to see how trees recycle energy from the sun back into the soil.

Leaves on the forest floor return nutrients to the soil.

STEPS

1. Dig down a few inches through the layers of leaves to uncover the different stages of decay.
2. See if the different stages support different types and numbers of organisms.
3. Put samples from the top, middle, and bottom layers into sealable bags or other clear containers and take them home.
4. Fill a kitchen garbage bag with dry leaves.
5. Keep the small bags sealed and observe them for several weeks.

6. After a few weeks, open the bags and allow them to dry out.
7. Examine the contents.
8. Divide the dry leaves in the large bag into two watertight kitchen trash bags.
9. Keeping as much air as possible in one bag, tie it closed so no moisture can get in.
10. Add a quart of water to the other bag and, keeping as much air inside as possible, tie it off.
11. Put the bags in a warm, dark place for a month, then check and compare them.
12. Put a shovelful of dirt or moist leaf litter and a quart of water in the dry-leaf bag, mix it up, and close it off.
13. Check it in two weeks.
14. When you're finished with the experiments, put the leaves in your garden or on your compost pile.

Create a soil profile in the woods.

Take the Next Step

Soil in a deciduous forest differs from that in a typical backyard. Usually, the humus and litter layers in a forest are much deeper than those of a backyard, and the organisms contained are more varied and numerous. Soils in coniferous forests generally are not very fertile and have fewer earthworms and other organisms. One reason for this is the resins in the needles that make the soil too acidic for many organisms and slow the decay process.

Create an on-site soil profile to study the soil's makeup.

1. Select an area at least 10 feet from the nearest live tree. A spot near an old snag or a fallen tree may work well.
2. Dig a hole straight down at least a foot on one side and angled (about 45 degrees) on the other to allow a better view. You may have to try several times to find a spot without roots or rocks blocking the way.
3. Look for layers showing yearly harvests of fallen leaves. Forest soil usually shows four distinct layers: litter on top, then humus, then soil stained by organic material, then parent matter (such as clay or sandy soil) below that. Beneath the parent matter is bedrock.

   Can you recognize distinct layers? Sometimes the litter and humus levels are several feet thick. The litter layer is usually dry and hardly decomposed at all. The humus layer is moist and dark-colored. Soil below usually is lighter colored, having been stained by seeping water that is rich in organic matter.
4. Spread samples from each layer on a light-colored surface while you sift through them looking for grubs (beetle larvae) and other larvae, insects, worms, and other invertebrates.
5. Collect samples from each layer in plastic bags, and take them home to examine the contents.
6. Spread some samples in a moist environment, such as a terrarium. After a while, you may find ferns and fungi growing from spores hidden in the soil.

Find Out More

See Lynn M. Stone, *Temperate Forests* (Vero Beach, FL: Rourke Enterprises, 1989) (for young readers).

Tips and Tidbits

More than 90 percent of forests in the lower 48 states have been cut at least once. Around the country, there are a few pockets of original-growth forest—called ancient forests or old growth. The largest of these is in the Pacific Northwest. Smaller stands of trees are found in rugged areas that made logging impractical.

About a third of the United States is covered by forests.

Examinations of forest soils have revealed impressive numbers of organisms: a teaspoonful may hold some 5 billion bacteria and hundreds of thousands of algae and fungi.

Earthworms eating their way through forest soils process prodigious amounts of soil, producing more than 40 tons of castings (also known as dung, excrement, or poop) per acre. In addition to making nutrients more available, the worms keep the soil loose, so air is available for roots and organisms.

COLLECT MOSSES, FERNS, AND FUNGI

LEVEL: Pathfinder (low; about 1 hour)

SEASONS: Summer or fall

MATERIALS:
Plastic sandwich bags
Pocket knife or garden pruning shears
Garden trowel

OPTIONAL
Field guides to mosses, ferns, and fungi

INTRODUCTION

Most forest soils are moist and rich in nutrients, but little or no direct sunlight reaches the forest floor. Therefore, most plants growing on the forest floor in the so-called field layer are adapted to these special conditions. Some of the most common plants are mosses and ferns. Fungi are not plants, but they too are common in many forests, and they share some characteristics with ferns and mosses.

Unlike most plants, which must be pollinated, mosses, ferns, and fungi reproduce by spores. Mosses reproduce in two stages. The plants produce male and female cells. When male cells are ripe and damp, the moss releases them, some of which reach tiny tubes (the female sex organ). The male cell then travels down the tube, joins the female cell, and the two cells grow into a spore-producing oospore. In response to summer's drier air, the plants release their spores. If conditions are favorable, the spores will turn into delicate, branching protonema, which in turn produce new moss plants.

In ferns, spores develop in tiny, brown dots (sporangia) on the leaves. The spores are released in autumn, and if they land in a moist area, they develop into a prothallus, a small, heart-shaped disk with roots. This intermediate stage in the fern's life cycle produces both sperm and eggs. If the moisture is sufficient for the sperm to reach the egg and fertilize it, a new fern will grow.

Mushroom spores grow into tiny threads called hyphae. The combined filaments of one hypha are called mycelia. When two compatible mycelia join (and if conditions are right), they are able to produce a mushroom, which releases spores to begin the process anew.

Explore a forest and find some mosses, ferns, and fungi. Examine these specially adapted and delicate organisms.

STEPS

1. Collect several patches of moss, some fern fronds, and a few mushrooms, and take them home.
2. Put them inside a newly prepared terrarium (see activity, page 21) that has only sterile soil and/or peat on the layers of charcoal, and gravel. Don't add any other plants.
3. Water the terrarium and put it in indirect light.
4. Watch and record what grows.

Mushroom Spore Prints

Make spore prints, which help naturalists identify mushrooms. Find some unopened mushrooms, carefully put a few in a plastic collection bag, and take them home. Cut off the stem from the top (cap) and set the cap (rounded side up) on paper. Some spores are dark and some are light, so for best results, place one mushroom on dark and one on light paper. Cover with a coffee can or jar, where it won't be disturbed. After a few hours (or overnight), the mushroom cap should open and release its spores, leaving a delicate pattern. Remove the cap and carefully spray the pattern with art fixative at least three times. Be sure to wash your hands after handling wild mushrooms. If you can't find any mushrooms, buy some and use them. You can also use paint to print with mushroom tops or cross sections.

Tips and Tidbits

Mosses probably were among the first terrestrial plants. As the mosses, lichens, and liverworts thrived, created soil, and helped anchor it, other plants could develop, take root, and spread.

In addition to helping break down rocks, mosses filter and collect dust particles from the air that add to the soil layer.

Many commercial potting soils use sphagnum moss, because it acts like tiny sponges to absorb and hold moisture.

Spanish moss, which hangs from trees in the southern United States, is not moss at all, but a flowering epiphyte—a plant that takes most of its needed nutrients and water from the air. Spanish moss is a relative of the pineapple plant.

Mushrooms and mosses are common in most U.S. forests.

Do not collect any plants or other specimens from parks. If you are on private land, ask permission of the owner before collecting any samples. Wash your hands well after handling any mushrooms.

Masses of interconnected fungi in forest soils form some of the world's largest communities of organisms, with underground, microscopic threads extending for miles. Just an ounce of forest soil can contain more than a mile of filaments. The above-ground mushrooms and toadstools are simply the spore-spreading, reproductive fruit.

Giant puffballs—a kind of fungi—produce trillions of spores.

Beaches

Create Statements and Sculptures in the Sand

LEVEL: Pathfinder (low; 1 hour or more)

SEASONS: Late spring, summer, and early fall

MATERIALS:

Digging equipment: scoops, shovels, buckets, etc.
Sculpting tools: spoon, stick, trowel, etc.
Ornaments: seaweed, driftwood, shells, pebbles, etc.
Trash collected from beach
Sunblock, wide-brimmed hat, and/or other protections from the sun

OPTIONAL

Photographs or illustrations of various animals

INTRODUCTION

What better way to while away the hours at the beach than building sandcastles? How about something more original? Don't just build castles in the sand, make a statement about something that counts, such as beach pollution.

Most of the trash on our beaches comes not from big ships or factories, but from individuals. These castaway items are not just bags, bottles, and broken sandals. A 1995 sweep of coastal areas by volunteer trash-pickers in 43 U.S. states and territories hauled in 80 chairs, along with televisions, mattresses, refrigerators, and freezers. The most common item, though, was cigarette butts, more than 800,000 of them.

Create an on-site environmental advertisement and/or wildlife sculpture. You'll challenge your creativity and maybe even spur a passerby to think twice about tossing that cigarette butt on the beach.

Creative sand sculptures can be pure fun, but they can also be a way to make people think about nature.

STEPS

1. Collect beach trash and incorporate it into a pollution-slamming sand sculpture. You could

create a giant ashtray and pile cigarette butts into it, sculpt a crab cleanup crew, or a school of trash-eating fish. Before you leave, be sure to bag the trash and throw it away.

2. If you're lucky enough to find yourself on a trash-free beach, build sand sculptures of sea turtles, pelicans, manatees, dolphins, or other coastal creatures. First draw an outline in the sand and then pile on sand as you bring your sculpture to life. This activity is sure to be a hit with the beachcombers.
3. If sculpture isn't your strong suit, collect natural beach materials and trash and take them back to the cottage or hotel and make a "Keep the Beach Clean" collage. This is a great rainy-day activity.

Find Out More

See the **Resources** listing, page 128.

Tips and Tidbits

Do your part: avoid walking on fragile sand dunes, which protect buildings from high tides, provide habitat for dune-dwellers, and reduce erosion.

For interesting sculpture-enhancing objects, investigate the strand line—the material left at the high-water mark as the tide recedes. This often contains an assortment of seaweed, grasses, wood, whelk egg cases, skate cases, crab shells and claws, and small insects or tiny, jumping sandhoppers, among other finds.

Like most habitats, beaches are fragile habitats and should be treated with respect.

Adorn your sculptures with drippy sandcastle towers. Use fine sand in a bucket of water (or if you're close to the water's edge, just dig down till water fills your hole). Grab a handful of sand and water and hold it like a claw. Let the watery sand drip off your downward-pointing fingertips. With practice and the right sand, you can build wonderfully tall, thin turrets. This is also a good method for making wild strands of seaweedlike hair.

Not counting cigarette butts, plastics are the most abundant trash item found along beaches and waterways, accounting for more than half of all trash found in recent cleanups. The next most common items are paper, metal, and glass. The most dangerous trash items for wildlife are bits of net, fishing line, rope, and straps that entangle birds and other animals. The 1995 Coastal Cleanup found nearly 160 entangled animals, only 14 of which could be released. One of these survivors was a coyote in Texas.

Make Waves in a Bottle

LEVEL: Pathfinder (low; about 15 minutes)

SEASONS: All

MATERIALS:

Liter soda bottle (or long, narrow bottle) with cap or cork (the ideal bottle would be long and square- or rectangular-shaped, rather than cylin drical)

Light-colored oil, such as canola or safflower

Water

Food color

OPTIONAL

Sand (well-rinsed) and small shells

Shifting sands play havoc with our best-laid plans.

INTRODUCTION

Waves are one of nature's magical wonders. Influenced by wind, tides, storms, beach slope, and other factors, they well up from the ocean with tremendous force and throw themselves at our feet. Waves can be a source of great pleasure. Their rhythmic sound and motion can be hypnotic, and they can carry body surfers and other wave-riders along with them.

But these natural wonders also can be destructive. Waves are coastal agents of erosion, moving great quantities of sand hither and thither. This is a natural process, but sometimes it conflicts with human processes, such as building and tourism. Every year, resort beaches spend millions of dollars to shore up their beaches and replenish lost sand or remove excess. In some coastal areas, lighthouses now stand in deep water or have been moved back from the shore in response to beach erosion.

When hurricanes or other violent storms blow, waves may batter and destroy man-made coastal structures. Sometimes earthquakes produce tidal waves that can be hundreds of feet high and travel at speeds greater than 500 miles an hour.

Humans can do little to stop the destructive potential inherent in such forces of nature. We can, however, learn from our mistakes. That means erecting buildings farther away from the ocean or behind protective dunes.

STEPS

For preparation, spend some time listening to the waves with your eyes closed. Let your mind drift out to sea and allow whatever images arise to float freely through your mind. Meditating to the sounds of waves can be relaxing and refreshing.

After a while, open your eyes and try focusing them on a single spot in the surf. It's not easy to do, because the surface waters are constantly moving. Sometimes it helps to focus your eyes beyond the surface, so the waves themselves become blurred. These activities are sometimes easier to pursue when there are few people on the beach, such as early in the morning or on a moonlit night. If the beach you're visiting faces east, make a family trip to watch the sunrise over the ocean.

After you've spent some time studying and appreciating waves, make a wave bottle to take home with you. Then you'll always have a reminder of the power and beauty of waves.

1. Fill a bottle about two-thirds with water (dyed blue or blue green) and a thin layer of clean, well-washed sand (if desired). You may also want to toss in a few small seashells and some glitter.
2. Fill the bottle the rest of the way with oil and seal it.
3. Allow the oil and water to separate completely, then rock it back and forth to simulate wave action. It's also fun to shake the contents and watch how the liquids separate. Sometimes, bits of sand will weigh down bubbles of oil, holding them below the water.

Even if it doesn't look exactly like a wave, the bottles make attractive window ornaments, and the movement of the liquids is relaxing—even hypnotic—to watch.

A wave bottle is relaxing to play with.

Waves are one of the best parts of the beach. Their rhythmic work gradually changes the coastal landscape..

Find Out More

See Janice VanCleave, *Janice VanCleave's Oceans for Every Kid* (New York: John Wiley & Sons, 1996).

Tips and Tidbits

It's not unusual for waves in some parts of Hawaii to reach a height of 40 feet or more.

If your sand isn't well rinsed, both the oil and water will soon become cloudy. Sooner or later the oil will become cloudy, in which case, it's time to make a new wave bottle.

Just a few inches below the surface sand and the crashing waves, moisture permeating through the sand keeps the subsurface temperature fairly constant.

Salt marshes around coastal areas are important growing-up (or staging) areas, where small fish and crustaceans find safety from larger underwater predators. For this reason, many shorebirds and wading birds gather in the marshes, looking for this abundant food source.

FULL-SCALE FISH PRINTING

LEVEL: Pathfinder (low; about 1 hour)

SEASONS: All

MATERIALS:

Whole, fresh fish (head, scales, and all) and/or shrimp, seaweed, etc. (flatter fish, such as flounder, perch, bass, grouper, and rockfish work best)
Thick, water-based ink or linoleum block-printing ink (preferably dark colors of red, green, blue, or brown); tempura paints will also work
At least one very small brush (size 00) and a 1" brush
Newsprint or other paper, about 8" × 10"(other papers that work well for fish printing include strong tissue paper, rice paper, sumi-e paper)
Newspapers (to protect your work area)
Modeling clay or paper and tape

OPTIONAL
Straight pins
Old toothbrush

INTRODUCTION

Fish printing (or rubbing) is an Asian art dating to the early 1800s. The proper name for this art form is gyotaku (pronounced *gio-ta'-koo*).

Whether you land a whopper while surf fishing or buy it from the market, fish rubbing allows you to see fish in a new light and to gain appreciation for their structure. If you have the right paints (permanent cloth colors), you can also make attractive and unusual T-shirts. Fish-rubbing techniques can also be used to make prints of shells, flowers, and other natural objects.

STEPS

(The following is adapted from the University of California Division of Agriculture and Natural Resources Leaflet 2548.)

1. Wash the fish with soap and water and wipe it dry, so the paint will stick to it better.
2. Spread out some newspapers and place the fish on them.
3. Use clay or rolled paper taped together to support the fins. You may want to use straight pins to hold the fins open.
4. Using a brush, apply paint or ink in a thin coat, first working from head to tail. Don't paint the

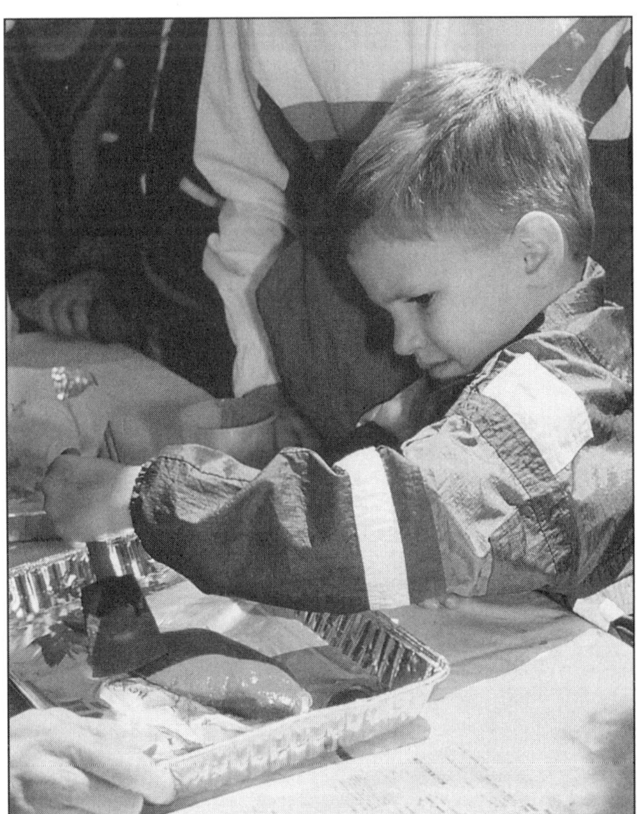

Children participate in a fish-printing workshop at a Virginia Beach marine science museum.

eye, which can be filled in with a brush after printing.

5. When the entire side of the fish is covered, reverse direction, making brushstrokes from tail to head. This will load the color around and under the scales, which makes for a better print. If you get some color on the underlying newspaper, cover it with a piece of paper before printing.
6. Carefully place the printing paper over the fish, and with a minimum of wrinkling or paper movement, rub the paper with your fingertips.
7. Gently lift the paper, starting at the head and peeling it back.
8. If the print worked well, it should be fairly detailed, except for the eye. Paint it in by hand.
9. For a more attractive picture, add details that didn't print well and embellish it with color—fin and tail highlights, stripes, bubbles, and a background color or seaweed landscape. Don't worry if your first print isn't that great; fine art takes practice. You can use the same fish several times. Simply reapply the color and make another print or wash the fish again, wipe it off, and start over.

Before you lift the paper from the fish, try some of the techniques learned in the leaf-printing activity (see page 78). Turn the fish and paper over, take an old toothbrush or a hard-bristle brush, dip it in colors, and use a stick, your finger, or a bit of screen to splatter paint around the fish, creating a silhouette around the print. Use green and blue for a watery look, or go wild with orange, red, yellow, and other bright colors and combinations. An excellent technique is to apply color to the finished print by dabbing it on with a sponge. Once you become a proficient fish printer, try making a mural.

Your first fish prints may not look this good, but with practice, you'll get the hang of it.

Find Out More

See Gwen Diehn and Terry Krautwurst, *Nature Crafts for Kids: 50 Fantastic Things to Make with Mother Nature's Help* (New York: Sterling Publishing Co., 1992); and Laurie Carlson, *Eco Art: Earth-Friendly Art & Craft Experiences for 3- to 9-Year-Olds* (Charlotte, VT: Williamson Publishing, 1993).

Tips and Tidbits

If you want to remove the fish's insides, go ahead, but stuff the cavity with newspaper or clay afterward for easier printing and don't scale the fish or cut off its head or fins.

Use fish-printing techniques with fabric paint to decorate T-shirts, aprons, tablecloths, curtains, or wall hangings.

Try printing with just the tail to make abstract designs.

Make a wall hanging to display your print. Glue the top end around a thin dowel or bamboo piece that is ½ inch or so longer than the print is wide. Do the same on the bottom end to add weight. Hang the print using string or yarn.

After you finish printing, wash the fish thoroughly before cleaning and cooking it.

Sand Casting

LEVEL: Naturalist (medium; about ½ hour)

SEASONS: Spring, summer, fall, and mild winter

MATERIALS:
Plaster of Paris
Water (tap or saltwater)
Mixing bucket
Acrylic paint and brush

OPTIONAL
Digging tools: sticks, spoons, shells
Old toothbrush
Sandpaper
Artist's knife or other sharp tool

INTRODUCTION

Let nature provide your workplace and inspiration. The moist sand near the ocean water is the perfect spot to do sand casting. All you need is some plaster of Paris and a good imagination, and you can make unique keepsakes of your trip to the beach.

STEPS

1. Dig out designs or faces in the firm sand. Don't make them larger than about a foot tall or wide, because the plaster will be more likely to break. Start simple, and work up to more complicated sculptures.

   Also, remember how the cast will come out—facing down, so to speak. If you are making a face or mask, the nose should be dug down into the sand, not sticking up toward you. Think of what you would get if you stuck your face into the sand (which is a possibility, if you don't mind getting sand in your face).
2. When the mold is finished, mix the plaster according to the instructions. The consistency should be that of honey. Plaster hardens quickly, so you have to work fast.
3. Pour the mixed plaster into the mold till it's halfway full.
4. For added strength, put in some small sticks before filling the rest of the mold with plaster.
5. Depending on conditions, the cast should be dry and hard within 15 minutes to half an hour. Carefully dig it out and allow it to dry for at least two hours.
6. When it's completely dry, use an old toothbrush to remove embedded sand.
7. Use fine sandpaper to smooth surfaces and a sharp tool or knife to refine or add details.
8. Paint with acrylic colors and add a final, clear coating for added protection.

Tips and Tidbits

For larger sculptures, combine one part plaster with one part sand mix (a kind of cement). This will produce a stronger, longer-lasting sculpture.

If you mix the plaster of Paris with seawater it will harden faster than it does with tap water.

Incorporate stones or seashells into your mold or glue them onto your cast when it is dry.

You can make casts of seashells as well. Put the shell at the bottom of a shallow depression in the sand, pour plaster in, let it set, and remove the cast and the shell.

Further Reading

The following is a selection of some of the excellent outdoor activity and other nature books that might interest you and/or your children. These are in addition to the books related to specific activities that are mentioned in the **FIND OUT MORE** sections.

Allison, Linda. *The Sierra Club Summer Book.* San Francisco: Sierra Club Books; Boston: Little, Brown and Co., 1989.

Berger, Melvin. *Outdoor Science Adventures.* New York: Scholastic, 1994.

Bonnet, Robert L., and G. Daniel Keen. *Environmental Science: 49 Science Fair Projects.* New York: McGraw-Hill, 1990.

Conrad, Jim. *Discover Nature in the Garden: Things to Know and Things to Do.* Mechanicsburg, PA: Stackpole Books, 1996.

Cornell, Joseph. *Sharing Nature by Children.* Nevada City, CA: Dawn Publications, 1979.

———. *Sharing the Joy of Nature.* Nevada City, CA: Dawn Publications, 1989.

Duensing, Edward. *Talking to Fireflies, Shrinking the Moon: A Parent's Guide to Nature Activities.* New York: Plume/Penguin Books, 1990.

Durrell, Gerald. *The Amateur Naturalist.* New York: Alfred A. Knopf, 1982.

Elkington, John, Julia Hailes, Douglas Hill, and Joel Makower. *Going Green: A Kid's Handbook to Saving the Planet.* New York: Puffin Books, 1990.

Harlow, Rosie, and Gareth Morgan. *175 Amazing Nature Experiments.* New York: Random House, 1991.

Harrison, Kit, and George Harrison. *America's Favorite Backyard Wildlife: An Intimate Look at the Fascinating Lives of Your Best-Loved Backyard Neighbors.* New York: Simon & Schuster, 1985.

Hunken, Jorie. *Ecology for All Ages.* Old Saybrook, CT: Globe Pequot Press, 1994.

Lingelbach, Jenepher, ed. *Hands-On Nature: Information and Activities for Exploring the Environment with Children.* Woodstock, VT: Vermont Institute of Natural Science, 1986.

Milord, Susan. *The Kids' Nature Book: 365 Indoor/Outdoor Activities and Experiences.* Charlotte, VT: Williamson Publishing, 1989. Part of a series of excellent nature books.

Petrash, Carol. *Earthways: Simple Environmental Activities for Young Children.* Mt. Ranier, MD: Gryphon House, 1992.

Potter, Jean. *Nature in a Nutshell for Kids: Over 100 Activities You Can Do in Ten Minutes or Less.* New York: John Wiley & Sons, 1995.

Sheehan, Kathryn, and Mary Waidner. *Earth Child: Games, Stories, Activities, Experiments & Ideas About Living Lightly on Planet Earth.* Tulsa: Council Oak Books, 1991.

Smith, Alison. *The Kids' Nature Almanac: Great Outdoor Discoveries and Activities for Parents and Children.* New York: Crown Trade Paperbacks, 1995.

Soucie, Gary. *Natural Fun: The NatureLink® Family Activity Book.* Vienna, VA: National Wildlife Federation, 1996.

Stein, Sara. *Noah's Garden: Restoring the Ecology of Our Own Back Yards.* Boston: Houghton Mifflin Co., 1993.

Tilgner, Linda. *Let's Grow! 72 Gardening Adventures with Children.* Pownal, VT: Storey Communications, 1988.

VanCleave, Janice Pratt. *Janice VanCleave's 200 Gooey, Slippery, Slimy, Weird & Fun Experiments.* New York: John Wiley & Sons, 1993. Part of an excellent series of books.

Western Regional Environmental Education Council. *Project Wild.* Houston, TX: 1985. Part of a nationwide environmental education program.

Resources

Outdoor Composting

Send a self-addressed envelope to the publishers, and they will send you their composting pamphlet. Write to Rodale Press, *Organic Gardening* magazine, "Five Steps to Quick Composting" pamphlet, 33 E. Minor St., Emmaus PA 18098.

Worm Composting

Mary Appelhof (the Worm Woman of Kalamazoo), *Worms Eat My Garbage: How to Set Up and Maintain a Worm Composting System* (Kalamazoo, MI: Flower Press, 1982). She also cowrote *Worms Eat Our Garbage,* a classroom curriculum. Both books (along with worms, bins, and other products) are available from Flowerfield Enterprises, 10332 Shaver Road, Kalamazoo MI 49002, or call 616-327-0108.

Indoor Gardening

"Garbage Garden," made by the Applewood Seed Company in Golden, Colorado, is an activity kit for turning everyday kitchen scraps into houseplants. It comes in a plastic garbage can container, along with tips for growing carrot tops, potato vines, a popcorn forest, and other projects. Look for it in bookstores, gift shops, and garden centers, or order it from Insect Lore by calling 800-548-3284.

Butterfly Gardening

The Young Entomologists' Society publishes a directory of insect zoos, butterfly houses, museums, and insect fairs in North America. Visit their home page on the World Wide Web at http://insects.ummz.lsa.umich.edu/yes/yes.html or send E-mail to YESbugs@aol.com, or send a self-addressed, stamped envelope requesting a free copy of "Gardening for Butterflies"(Minibeast Factsheet No. 5), a "Bibliography" of Butterfly Gardening Information, and membership details to Y.E.S., 1915 Peggy Place, Lansing MI 48910-2553.

Y.E.S. also has a Minibeast Merchandise catalog listing hundreds of informative books, brochures, guides, games, models, and other invertebrate items.

Papillon Distributors sells caterpillars, cocoons, and chrysalises of several moth and butterfly species. Write them at The Butterfly Place, 120 Tyngsboro Road, Westford MA 01886-4995, or call 508-392-0955.

Create a schoolyard or community butterfly garden. America the Beautiful Fund offers seeds and a "Green Earth Guide" for large-scale projects. The seeds—donated from seed companies—are from the previous year, but they have an 85 percent germination rate. Send a self-addressed, stamped envelope to America the Beautiful Fund, 219 Shoreham Building, Washington DC 20005. Or send $15, along with a project description and name of the project leader, to the above address to receive the guide and 120 flower and vegetable packets. Add $5 for 30 extra packages—ask for butterfly, herb, and wildflower seeds.

For a list of butterfly showplaces in the United States and abroad, send a self-addressed, stamped envelope and a request to The Xerces Society, 4828 SE Hawthorne Blvd., Portland OR 97215.

To subscribe to *Butterfly Gardeners' Quarterly* newsletter, write to PO Box 30931, Seattle WA 98103. For a sample copy, send S.A.S.E.

Applewood Seed Company makes a kit, "Fantasy Garden: Beautiful Flowers That Butterflies Love," with marigold, zinnia, and phlox seeds and plans for creating a butterfly-shaped garden. Look for it in bookstores, gift shops, and garden supply stores, or order it from Insect Lore by calling 800-548-3284.

Pole-Bean Tepee/Gardening

The nonprofit National Gardening Association publishes a monthly news magazine and can help answer your gardening questions. Join by writing them at NGA, 180 Flynn Ave., Burlington VT 05401, or call 802-863-1308.

Gourds

The American Gourd Society sells books and a video about gourds, and it publishes a quarterly newsletter, *The Gourd.* For membership information and a publications list, send a self-addressed, stamped envelope or 32-cent stamp with request to AGS, PO Box 274, Mt. Gilead OH 43338.

The Purple Martin Conservation Society offers a 10-page gourd booklet, *Growing Gourds and Preparing Gourd Homes for Martins,* for about $3 ($5 with seeds). Write them at PMCS, Edinboro University of Pennsylvania, Edinboro PA 16444, or call 814-734-4420.

Birdhouse

Go all out! Plan a bluebird trail along a scenic drive, or in a golf course, cemetery, scenic drive, or other open area. Contact the North American Bluebird Society for books, birdhouse plans, and other information: NABS, Box 6295, Silver Spring MD 20916-6295.

Building birdhouses is just one way to help nesting birds. In addition to providing mud for platform-nesting birds (see activity on page 40), put out a bundle of nesting materials. Stuff a plastic mesh bag (the kind that onions and oranges sometimes come in) or a suet holder with cotton; hair; fur; short bits of string, thread, yarn, cloth, or used dental floss; or anything else that birds might use. You can also just set these materials out in an open box, in a location protected from lurking cats.

Birdhouses for tree swallows, wrens, chickadees, bluebirds, and titmice can be made from large, dried bottle gourds, also known as dipper gourds, and even birdhouse gourds (see Grow Some Gourds activity, page 28). The gourd should be about 4 inches in diameter. Cut a 1½-inch hole with a drill saw or keyhole saw at least 5 inches above the base, and remove the insides. Drill two ¼-inch or smaller holes at the top of the gourd for a string or wire and hang it in a tree.

Bird Feeder

The National Bird-Feeding Society has declared February to be National Wild Bird Feeding Month. The organization publishes *The Bird's-Eye reView,* a bimonthly newsletter on bird feeding and housing, and it offers an activity kit for parents and other educators. Send a self-addressed, stamped envelope to NBS, PO Box 23, Northbrook IL 60065-0023.

Every winter a dedicated army of 12,000 birdwatchers keeps track of the feathered friends that frequent their feeders. They report the kinds and numbers of birds to Project FeederWatch at the Cornell Laboratory of Ornithology. This helps the number-crunchers there monitor winter migration movements and keep tabs on local populations. Many programs are run by teachers in schools across the country. The Lab's Common Feeder Birds poster costs $2. Cornell publishes *Living Bird* magazine, a quarterly newsletter entitled *Birdscope,* and its Crow's Nest Birding Shop sells CDs, nest boxes, feeding and watching equipment, and books. Visit their home page at http://www.ornith.cornell.edu/, call 800-843-2473, send E-mail to birdeducation@cornell.edu, or write to Cornell Lab of Ornithology, Project FeederWatch, 159 Sapsucker Road, Ithaca NY 14850.

The Canada connection for Project FeederWatch is Bird Studies Canada, Long Point Bird Observatory, Project FeederWatch, Box 160, Port Rowan, Ontario NOE IMO, Canada; or call 519-586-3531.

The American Birding Association concentrates on birding beyond the backyard. In addition to adult-oriented publications, the group publishes a quarterly newsletter for teen birdwatchers, *A Bird's-Eye View,* and offers student discounts. For membership information, call them at 800-850-2473.

Bird feeding is widely practiced, so tons of information sources on the activity are available, including books, pamphlets, brochures, and CD-ROMs. Even some encyclopedias have sections on the subject, with instructions for building bird feeders.

Baths

If you have the space and energy, consider creating a small pond for wildlife. Unless you have an abundant supply of clay, you'll need lots of sand or newspaper and heavy-duty plastic (PVC) pool liner. Then, all you need are rocks, edge plantings, a water source, and a strong back. You can use a hose as a water source, but since the pool will require a lot of water, you might be better off using rainwater from a cistern hooked to your downspout or, alternatively, a recirculating pump. This is a big job, but it can be very rewarding and can last for years.

A wildlife pond can be a great, natural-looking wildlife attraction.

Specially designed baths for birds are available from Avian Aquatics, 6 Point Circle, Lewes DE 19958, telephone 302-645-8643; and from Iron Design, Bird Baths, and Drippers, 26309 146th St., Zimmerman MN 55398, telephone 612-856-4700. Call or write to request a price list.

Gardening for the Birds

Gardening and bird-watching are two of the most popular outdoor activities, so there are many, many publications that discuss gardening for birds. The gardening section of your local library or bookstore should have information on specific plant species. Other good sources for information are the U.S. Fish and Wildlife Service, the local office of the federal Soil Conservation Service, wildlife and gardening magazines, and many wildlife conservation organizations, including the National Wildlife Federation.

For information about local or regional conditions and plant types, consult your local agricultural extension agent, state wildlife agency (many have nongame departments), state or local office of the federal Natural Resources Conservation Service, long-time gardeners, and employees at most garden supply stores.

Additional resources on the subject include Carol Henderson, *Landscaping for Wildlife* (St. Paul, MN: Minnesota Department of Natural Resources, 1994); Ruth Shaw Ernst, *The Naturalist's Garden* (Old Saybrook, CT: Globe Pequot Press, 1987); and John K. Terres, *Songbirds in Your Garden* (Chapel Hill, NC: Algonquin Books, 1994).

Gardening for Hummingbirds

Several companies make hummingbird-gardens-in-a-box (flower seeds, for the most part), sold in gift shops, bookstores, and garden supply stores. One of them is *Gardening on the Wing for Hummingbirds,* a Backyard Garden Kit, by Sally's Choice, Seattle, Washington, which comes with a feeder, seed-starting container, instructions, guide booklet, and seeds.

Make your own hummingbird food by mixing one cup refined sugar with four cups of water. Boil the mixture for two minutes, let it cool, and pour it into your feeder. Refrigerate any extra nectar.

Replace the nectar and clean the feeder every third day (more often if the days are really hot), or spoiled nectar may make your hummingbirds sick. To delay spoilage, hang your feeders out of direct sun. Soak your feeder for an hour in a solution of 2 ounces of bleach mixed with a gallon of water, rinse well, and allow it to dry before refilling. Hummers also like fruit flies, so hang a mesh bag with old bananas or cantaloupe near the feeder.

If ants invade, try a new location or put Vaseline on the attachment string. Other visitors may come to your feeder, including butterflies, yellow jackets, bumblebees, moths, and even some other birds. Put out several feeders if the hummingbirds mob and fight over your single feeder.

Praying Mantis

You can buy praying mantis egg cases from mail-order companies, many of which also sell live insects (such as ladybugs) that prey on common garden pests, parasites that attack harmful insects, and other nontoxic pest controls. One such company is Natural Pest Controls. To order a nest of about 300 praying mantis eggs, call 916-726-0855, or write to NPC, 8864 Little Creek Drive, Orangevale CA 95662.

Habitat for the Harmless

If you're not handy with tools, you can buy *The Bug Book and Bug Bottle,* by Dr. Hugh Danks (New York: Workman Publishing Co., 1987).

Bats

To order merchandise or request a catalog, write Bat Conservation International at PO Box 162603, Austin TX 78716-2603, or call 800-538-BATS. For more information or to join BCI, call 512-327-9721.

Simple bat house modifications: For increased protection, attach a 3 × 28-inch roof to the top. Bats welcome a longer landing lip (6 inches or so) at the bottom. Also, you can extend the house's height and width (side-to-side) by 1 and 2 feet, respectively, to accommodate more bats. Just be sure the interior space is ¾ to 1 inch, and add an inside, ¾-inch support in the middle for houses wider than 24 inches.

Observatory

Carolina Biological Supply sells vivaria complete with light hoods for warmth, foundation materials, water bowl, and instructions for set-up and use. You can even order one with a Woodhouse's toad, garter snake, or other inhabitant, which is shipped about two weeks after the vivarium arrives. For information, write them at CBS, 2700 York Road, Burlington NC 27215, or call 800-334-5551. Ask for their free catalog, *Carolina's K-8 Science Source.*

Adopt a Stream

Maryland Save Our Streams offers Adopt a Stream programs for adults and children. Their youth curriculum book, *Be Part of Something Big,* is free for in-state residents who attend a training seminar; postage is charged for out-of-state requests. For more information or an Adopt a Stream packet, call 800-448-5826 or send a self-addressed, stamped envelope to MSOS, 258 Scotts Manor Drive, Glen Burnie MD 21061. The Izaak Walton League of America has its own Save Our Streams program, with a *Hands-On SOS Teacher's Manual* and a video that parents and other educators can buy. Send a SASE with information request to IWLA, 707 Conservation Lane, Gaithersburg MD 20878. The league also has a technical information hotline for stream-related questions: 800-BUG-IWLA (284-4952).

River Watch Network helps thousands of waterway monitors with networking, technical support, publications, and workshops. Send SASE and a request for more information to RWN, 153 State

St., Montpelier VT 05602, call 802-223-3840, or E-mail them at rwn.igc.org. Similarly named, but different, River Network serves river-monitoring organizations. RN has an online database of more than 3,000 citizen groups nationwide. Find it via the network's home page on the World Wide Web at http://www.rivernetwork/~ rivernet.

Racing Waters

The U.S. Environmental Protection Agency Water Office has a home page on the Internet at http://www.epa.gov/ow. It includes an abridged list of hundreds of volunteer water-monitoring groups around the country as well as information about EPA publications on streams, lakes, and wetlands. Regional EPA offices also offer many publications. EPA Region 10 has published *Streamwalk Manual.* If you live in Washington, Alaska, Oregon, or Idaho, you can order a free copy by calling EPA Region 10 at 800-424-4372. Outside those states, write NCEPI, 11029 Kenwood Road, Bldg. 5, Cincinnati OH 45242. EPA Region 10 also offers lake- and wetland-walk manuals.

Your state department of environmental quality may also be able to help you find a local waterway-monitor group to join. Serious stream sleuths will be interested in *The Volunteer Monitor,* a free, twice-yearly national newsletter for water-quality monitors. To subscribe, write to VM, 1318 Masonic Ave., San Francisco CA 94117, or call 415-255-8049.

Streamside Creature Survey

Wade more deeply into rivers and streams. Global Rivers Environmental Education Network will send you free information if you send a SASE and a request to GREEN, 721 East Huron St., Ann Arbor MI 48104, or call them at 313-761-8142, send E-mail to green@green.org, or contact their World Wide Web site at http://www.igc.apc.org/green.

GREEN also has two books that are particularly suited to use by parents: *Field Manual for Water Quality Monitoring* and *Investigating Streams and Rivers,* which is an ideal supplement to the field manual.

The Izaak Walton League of America offers an inexpensive 46-page booklet, *SOS Monitor's Guide to Aquatic Macroinvertebrates* (insect larvae and crustaceans). See the Adopt a Stream resources (page 126) for the league's telephone number, or order the guide from GREEN.

Aquatic Critter Collector

The Tennessee Valley Authority offers several booklets in its Water Quality Series, including *Water Quality Sampling Equipment, Homemade Sampling Equipment, Common Aquatic Flora and Fauna of the Tennessee Valley* (which also is applicable to many other areas), and *Organizing and Conducting a Cleanup on Public Lands and Waterways.* A stream monitoring manual is also in the works. To request a set, write TVA, WML CST 16D, 1101 Market St., Chattanooga TN 37402-2801, or call 423-751-7338.

Get Your Feet Wet

The Terrene Institute specializes in publications about water pollution in wetlands and other water bodies. They can also tell you about American Wetlands Month, an annual celebration in May. Write them at 4-B Herbert St., Alexandria VA 22305, or call 703-548-5473.

If you have wetlands questions call the Environmental Protection Agency's Wetlands Information Hotline at 800-832-7828, send E-mail to wetlands-hotline@epamail.epa.gov, or visit the EPA's home page at http://www.epa.gov/our. Use these to request free fact sheets on wetlands topics, as well as teacher curriculum guides, posters, and other information.

Wetland Model

Wade even deeper into wetlands—get the educator's guide, *WOW! The Wonders of Wetlands,* published by Environmental Concern, Inc., and The Watercourse. This comprehensive, 330-page, soft-cover book provides a short course in wetland issues, with activities for kids, grades K–12. Write to Environmental Concern, PO Box P, St. Michaels MD 21663-0480, or call them at 410-745-9620.

National Wetland Inventory Maps of many areas are available through the U.S. Geologic Survey at a modest price. Call 800-USA-MAPS for more information.

Dead Snags and Rotting Logs

Project Learning Tree supplies teachers and other educators in all 50 states with activity and craft ideas aimed at levels pre-K through 12. For information, write the American Forest Foundation, 111 19th St. NW, Suite 780, Washington DC 20036.

Statements in Sand

Every year on the third Saturday of September, people around the country volunteer their time and energy to clean up beaches, streams, parks, and other public places. Their efforts not only make these areas look better, they make them safer for people and wildlife. The 1995 U.S. Coastal Cleanup involved more than 130,000 volunteers at about 3,000 U.S. locations and covered almost 6,000 miles of shoreline and waterways. In three hours, workers picked up 4 million pieces of trash with a combined weight of more than 2.5 million pounds.

In 10 years, some 80,000 volunteers have netted and bagged nearly 3 million pounds of trash just in North Carolina. Two activity booklets are available through the University of North Carolina Sea Grant Program to help inform kids about the dangers of trash to people and wildlife: *Splish-Splash: A Big Sweep Aquatic Primer,* for ages 5–7, and *Ripples: A Big Sweep Elementary Activity Guide,* for educators. Send $3 ($2 for North Carolina residents) to NC Big Sweep, PO Box 908, Raleigh NC 27602-0908, or call 800-27SWEEP (277-9337), or 919-828-6686. To find out about annual cleanup efforts in your area, call 800-CMC-BEACH, leave your name and address, and the Center for Marine Conservation will send you an information packet.

Index

Page numbers in *italics* indicate illustrations